FRESH
ANGELS
—AND—
MARKINGS

M.S. LYNCH

FRESH ANGELS AND MARKINGS

ARPress

ILLUMINATING IDEAS,
EMPOWERING VOICES

ARPress
45 Dan Road Suite 5
Canton MA 02021

Hotline: 1(888) 821-0229
Fax: 1(508) 545-7580

Ordering Information:
Quantity sales. Special discounts are available on quantity purchases by corporations, associations, and others. For details, contact the publisher at the address above.

Printed in the United States of America.

ISBN-13:   Softcover   979-8-89330-761-0
               eBook   979-8-89330-762-7

Library of Congress Control Number: 2024903475

TABLE OF CONTENTS

FOREWORD TO FRESH ANGELS AND MARKINGS

A "reluctant Christian" seems somehow more authentic to me. Mike Lynch was drawn into service to his faith while nurturing plans for a completely different life. I met him when I joined the faculty at the middle school where he was teaching eighth grade language arts and American history. I was impressed by his calmness, his pragmatism, and his general goodness. Having the same lunch period for thirteen years gave us time to become friends.

At some point, he shared with me some of his life stories. "Angels? You actually saw them?" Having had some of my own experiences with divine intervention, I was able to take him at his word. As we approached retirement, he told me of his plans to write a book about his spiritual journey. I said, "I would read that book."

Eventually, his book was written. At teacher get-togethers, he would talk about needing a typist. About the third time he brought this up, I could tell he was feeling some anxiety about it.

I asked, "How many pages?"

"About 120."

"I could do that."

"Really?"

So, I typed. I edited. I removed many exclamation points and advised on sentence construction. I retyped. I footnoted. I took on more than I bargained for. I read this book like no one else ever will. I absorbed it. In the process, I saw how deeply spiritual this man is. I asked him once, "Why he wasn't one of those proselytizing Christians." He said, "Because I have been through the dark night of the soul." There were about fifteen years when he struggled to find a position as a pastor. Why couldn't he? I wondered aloud if the professors at his seminary had given him a poor recommendation because he had not completely embraced their interpretation of theology but stayed true to his evangelical beliefs. That idea took him completely by surprise. That cynical possibility had never occurred to him.

Of course, there was much more to it than that. Only when I was immersed in his story did I come to understand his reluctance to be a "Christian." The young Mike saw the institutional church lacking in the power of the Holy Spirit, signs and wonders, angels, and prophecy. The church had much smoke but little fire. Only as I read his stories did I come to understand the powerful influence of a deeply spiritual childhood, the introspective and reflective nature that caused him to keep detailed spiritual journals for over forty years, and the intellectual curiosity that led to careful study of the writings of the mystics, Teresa of Avilla and St. John of the Cross. Mike quoted to me from Thomas Merton, another strong influence upon him: "Meditation has no point and no reality unless it is firmly rooted in life."

Fresh Angels and Markings shares personal experiences of God's actions upon Christians firmly rooted in life. It uses personal experiences to express a contemplative call to follow Jesus in this time. Instead of going on monastic retreats, one must invade the world with love, mercy, and good works that Jesus did as recorded in the Gospels.

When we were nearly finished, I asked Mike if, when he was talking about needing a typist, he was hoping that I would do it. He was shocked. "No! I was surprised. I prayed and prayed about it." I had to laugh. This was truly the only time I had ever been the answer to someone's prayers! It has been an honor to work on this book with Mike. I think of St. Paul, knocked off his horse by a light brighter than the sun and called upon to profess his new-found faith, only doing what he did because sometimes God will not take "no" for an answer, no matter how reluctant the Christian may be.

Dorothy Schleif Nicolas

ACKNOWLEDGMENT

This book would not have been possible without the role of spiritual and philosophical mentors in my life.

Glenn Matt, the Campus Crusade director at Western Michigan University, taught me the importance of journaling because God is an exciting, creative Lord and therefore my life will be full and meaningful.

At Seattle Pacific University I was a student in philosophy under Dr. Walter Johnson. Dr. Johnson gave me the tools to think critically and guided me to the Christian mystical tradition and especially Rufus Jones, the great Quaker mystic.

My mother, Thelma Foresteen Lynch, was my early model of a godly woman who was a dreamer of dreams and a Christian of great depth. My wife of forty-seven years, Jane, who named the angels that I saw and who shared in the visions and words of knowledge from the Holy Spirit that have guided us all these years. This list of luminaries would be incomplete without Dr. Robert A. Pitman who was my theological mentor and friend while I served an internship at the First Presbyterian Church of San Mateo, California from 1979-1980.

The person who really helped me edit and rewrite this memoir is a teacher friend, Dory Schleif Nicolas. Dory not only retyped the entire manuscript of 49,000 words but she also edited grammar and sentence structure. She is the one who said, "I would read this book," before it was finished!

Also, I would like to acknowledge the help for the book's cover, a watercolor was from an artist friend, Robin Dolarian, who painted this airbrush picture of the cross with a straw while waiting for a kidney transplant that saved his life.

M. S. Lynch

Book Synopsis

Acquisitions editor

Re.: Author Reputation Press LLC

By: Michael Lynch

Date: November 4, 2022

There is a great interest in the world today regarding angels and how they function in the Kingdom of God. I decided to write a memoir covering fifty-five years of my life. I used personal journals and diaries that I kept since my college days. In these journals I wrote about my life and my experience with God and with the supernatural.

The theme of the book containing 21 chapters is how the Holy Spirit interacts with ordinary people to do extraordinary things. Since half of my career was spent with serious criminal inmates in Alameda County, California, I have included this material in my book. I have added biblical theology where it was needed but avoided a "preachers tone" which I never did anyway. My presupposition is that Jesus still reveals himself to those who diligently seek him!

In my life I began my Christian walk out of a neo-pagan lifestyle. My conversion experience at Western Michigan University was not by man or any Christian witness but by the Spirit of Christ in a revelation to me as a twenty-year-old student. The book contains various friends and family members who have experienced God in: dreams, visions, scripture, prayer and signs and wonders.

The book was a year in writing and editing. I first began the memoir fifteen years ago, but I put it down and eventually lost the manuscript. I am glad that I lost it now as so much more has happened to me since then!

I have written twenty-one chapters and approximately 50,000 words. I wrote it for an audience of people who are seeking to go deeper into God as Christians and also to those who are spiritually hungry for "something more."

Michael Lynch

I
Kingdom in the North

"You will seek me and find me
if you seek me
with all your heart." (Jer. 29:13)

As a young boy between the ages of eight and ten, I had the same recurring dream. These dreams are what the psychiatrist Carl Jung called "great dreams." My grandmother, Sadie Zoppelli, and my mother, Thelma Lynch, were dreamers. They believed that dreams are a form of ancient, precognitive language that the Spirit of God uses to speak to people today.

My mother kept a thick, aging dream book of symbols and meanings or archetypes. We often shared our dreams and searched for the meanings of the dreams in the well-used book. I was frequently reminded of Joseph in the book of Genesis as a "dreamer of dreams" and a biblical character who could interpret dreams with God's help.

My recurring dream was my solace at night. I dreamed of a faraway place where I was a pilgrim traveler to a far north country. In the realm of medieval mansions and banners that fluttered in the wind, I was a small boy of no rank or privilege. Yet I was in this vast and mighty empire that was without end or beginning. Banners of royalty flapped in the breeze that constantly blew in the kingdom. Everything had great vitality and energy emanating from a central source. That source of power and life was the throne of God.

I stood in the presence of a mighty king not of this Earth, but I could never see his face. I felt very small and lowly, like a squire to a great lord. I did not know as a child that no man could see God's face and live. Even Moses was hidden in the cleft of a rock when YHWH passed by him on the mountain of God. Curiously, I did not see other creatures or angels in this beautiful place in the north. This God who dwelt there in my dreams was a benevolent Father and was full of love.

At the same time, he was "awe-full" and transcendent. The psalmist would declare his majesty:

> "The Lord is high above the nations. His glory (Kabod) above the Heavens. Who is like the Lord our God, who dwells on high who humbles himself to behold the things that are in the heavens and in the earth?"[1]

Between the years 1959 and 1961, I dreamed great dreams of this high place in the Mountains of the North. I loved going there in my night vigils. This kingdom was a place of peace and harmony. That same year, my grandmother Sadie died. She had lived on a ranch in Nebraska and had helped my mother out financially. She was a wise and spiritual person, having been baptized in the Swedish missionary church at the age of ten. Sadie was a follower of the prophetess, Ellen G. White of the Seventh Day Adventist movement. Her most treasured book besides the bible was *The Great Controversy* by Ellen White. I read this book after my birth in Christ.

Perhaps my bed-wetting phase had something to do with my Nana's death and my mother's great sadness. My mother, Thelma, had a mystical experience of Jesus holding her heart during her grief. Thelma told me that "Jesus seemed to seize my heart and hold it, and a great peace came upon me, but it was a very frightful experience!" This happened to her suddenly in the depths of her despair in 1959. I was only eight years old, and I slept so soundly and dreamed so deeply that I could not wake up. I also walked in my sleep, which caused my mother great dismay, and she worried about me.

During this same period of time, I began to realize that my father was "out of his mind," and I could not trust him. My mother tried to explain to us that he was mentally ill, but to me as a child, he seemed mean and cruel. Bi-polar manic depression was not discussed, and even our family doctor would not refer Jeff to a psychiatrist. I felt like a fatherless orphan. Therefore, God became my Father.

I came of age at twelve years old and lost my innocence. I also quit dreaming of the Kingdom in the North. I was old enough to join the

---

[1] Ps. 113:4-6 NKJV.

American Baptist Church, of which my parents were charter members. The Rev. George Fish taught the catechism class to me and another boy after school for four weeks. Finally, the big day came, and I was fully immersed in the baptismal tank on the stage of the church. This allowed me to partake of Holy Communion once a month. For me, it was a huge rite of passage. I believed I would be a changed person. My belief system was more magical than biblical. I had been taught that the water and the declaration of my faith washed all my sins and debts away. I made sure to broadcast this news to my friend across the street, who was also named Mike. After keenly observing me for a month, Mike asked me, "How are you different from me?" I had no answer, as my old sin nature was in charge of my daily living. His question greatly bothered me, because I had expected a huge transformation to occur. Nothing happened. My mind was still dull to the voice of the Holy Spirit.

The only positive that I took away from being washed in the baptismal fount was that I quit wetting the bed. I began to experience my hormones and libido, and I felt somewhat normal. My adolescent doubts concerning God increased, but I still prayed my nightly prayers as my mother had taught me. I helped my mother clean the church every Saturday for about four hours. I actually looked forward to this time of being alone in God's house. I had experienced God as "Holy Other," but as a twelve and thirteen year old child, I wanted a more personal relationship with this mysterious Being. I did not know anyone except my mother, Thelma, who had any kind of personal relationship with God.

Flint, Michigan, in the early 1960s was booming. It was the home of Buick. Since the "sit down strikes" in 1932, it was also the birthplace of the auto unions. All my friends' parents worked in the auto industry, as did my father. They were hardworking folks, and they also were a hard drinking lot and not very religious. The Roman Catholics seemed to be the predominant Christian group in our area. The Knights of Columbus and the other groups in the fraternal Catholic orders seemed to enjoy alcohol and had a lot of babies. Other than the statues of the saints and the incense and candles, I saw no difference in their practice of faith and mine. It all seemed like a "ghost dance" to me. In addition to this, my Catholic friends were wilder than the public school boys that I knew.

My school years at Bentley High were a blur of sports, dating, alcohol, and trips up north with my childhood friend Mike, who was becoming an alcoholic. I did take my girlfriend, Kathy, to church with me on Easter once, and she took me to her church in Flint. It was in a stone cathedral as cold as a Siberian winter. Kathy tried to civilize me, but cultural art shows and folk rock did not fill my void for the Living God. Sex became a "bacchanal god" of drunken parties for a period of time, but that too became passé. My neo-pagan lifestyle was further complemented by my admission to Western Michigan University in Kalamazoo, Michigan. Despite my dismal grade point average in high school, I managed to win a Michigan Higher Educational award that would pay for my books as long as I went to a college in Michigan. The college I attended was considered to be the third best school in the state after the University of Michigan and Michigan State.

My freshman year at WMU was full of action. The Vietnam War was causing the campus protests to increase. As I sat in the most boring class that I had ever taken, Sociology 101, the smell of tear gas wafted along Western Michigan Avenue as police and students battled it out in the street. I was not interested in violence and confrontation. I preferred smoking marijuana and hashish and dropping acid (LSD) to protesting. I was still trying to find God through psychedelics as Timothy Leary proclaimed: "Tune in, turn on, and drop out." I thought that was reality.

My grades improved in college because I valued my learning and appreciated the fact that my mother was paying my bills. While doing her dishes in the kitchen, which was her time of prayer and meditation, Thelma heard God say to her in the Spirit, "Apply for a teaching job at Barhitte Elementary School as they need teachers!" She was hired immediately and finished her one class to graduate from the University of Nebraska. After that, she worked on a master's degree as a reading specialist at Wayne State University in Detroit. So, mom, who was in her late 40s, and her prodigal son, Michael, were in school at the same time!

My mother was worried about me in a spiritual way. Her many prayers seemed to go unanswered as my sophomoric rebellion continued. I believed there was a God somewhere in the cosmos, but I thought he was unknowable. I did not connect Jesus with God except as a prophet or lesser deity. I was much more interested in the occult and drug movement pervading the 1960s. "Black Magic Woman" by Santana played on the jukebox every day in the student union building. Everybody was "getting high."

When summer rolled around, I found a job in the local mall selling men's clothes at A.M. Davison's. My previous summer work was at a steel foundry and AC Sparkplug factory in Flint. The clothing job paid a minimum wage of $1.65, but I did not come home looking like a coal miner. The late summer parties continued with drugs from Southeast Asia, compliments of our soldier friends in Vietnam. Not everyone went to college, but if a man did not have a military deferment, he was immediately drafted by the White Fathers of the local draft board. Thanks to a football injury to my knee as a high school senior, my draft rating was 1-Y, which meant "not available for the service unless a national emergency occurred." So even if I dropped out of college, they still could not draft me.

My parents were part of Richard Nixon's "Silent Majority." They were Republicans and voted for Nixon for president. Both of my parents smoked cigarettes, but neither of them drank alcohol. They did use many over-the-counter drugs however. Our kitchen had an entire cabinet full of prescribed drugs such as diet pills, painkillers, and lithium for my father's manic depression. They disapproved of me smoking pot that contained only one percent THC, but they were using much stronger drugs, legal opiates. Nevertheless, Jeff and Thelma were attentive parents, and my mother's love for me, my brother, and two sisters was felt deeply by all of us.

Just prior to WMU's classes resuming in the fall, I had a mystical experience. On August 24, 1970, I came home from a raucous party where I had used drugs and alcohol. It was the last party of the summer, so my friends and I made it count. I stumbled home at 3:00 a.m. and went to my bedroom to lie down and go to sleep. I was shocked to see my old King James Bible on the bed with the "Upper Room devotional" for that night underlined with a black marker. I could not sleep so I read the devotional.

"For the moment all discipline seems painful rather than pleasant but later it yields the peaceful fruits of righteousness to those who have been trained by it. Strengthen the hands that hang down and the weak and feeble knees lest the limb which is lame be not put out of joint but rather be healed."[2]

When I read these words, it was like a light exploded in my brain. Everything seemed to be clear, and my spiritual slumber seemed to disappear. I knew it was God in the Spirit speaking directly to my soul. I was intrigued thinking maybe this God of the bible still speaks today. I continued to read for an hour. I read the rest of Hebrews and also James. Finally, sleep overtook me. Someone or something had given me illumination of light in my dark world. I was immediately attracted to this "fruit of righteousness," but I did not understand what the bible meant by "conviction of sin, of righteousness and judgment to come." Righteousness to me was being truthful and doing one's best. But the bible spoke of righteousness as "God putting man in a right relationship with himself." Jesus also said, "Turn away from your sins, because the kingdom of heaven is near."[3]

I returned to college for my sophomore year full of confidence in my abilities. I had pledged the best fraternity on campus and had been accepted into Sigma Phi Epsilon. Most of their social functions were based on booze and parties. My roommate, Ron, was also in the fraternity. Ron was even more lost than I was. That year he got really involved with drugs and even sold them on campus, thanks to our overseas connection with soldiers in Vietnam. I was beginning to change, and the drug experience bored me. My best friend from high school, John, transferred to WMU and became my roommate. John

[2] Heb. 12:11-12 RSV
[3] Matt. 4:12b TEV.

followed in Ron's footsteps and "turned on" also. All of us had a heart-shaped vacuum in our lives that only God could fill. But the enemy, Satan, was glad to fill our lives with lies and false gods like drugs, rock 'n' roll, and sex.

When I returned to school, I tried to forget about my illumination by the Spirit. But the voice of God kept speaking to me in my head. I began to have a sense of dread that if I died, I would be condemned to hell. Where did this feeling of dread come from? I was not an existentialist consumed with existence over essence. If anything, I was an idealist and a dreamer. Nevertheless, the voice would not go away. I had no bible in my room and zero Christian's friends, and I did not attend church. I felt like I was being haunted, and a fear of death followed me.

I began to think that I was losing my mind like my father, the manic-depressive. But Jeff never heard voices or had hallucinations. I was under a heavy burden to surrender my life to this unseen God who was convicting me of my unrighteousness. God wanted me to take a leap of faith into his promises and not into the dark. But I was a materialist, and I wanted to be a lawyer and make a lot of money and marry a European woman and live abroad. That is why I was a pre-law major studying political science.

One beautiful autumn weekend, my roommates Ron and John drove home to Flint. I remained on campus to study. I was getting all As and Bs, and I had a serious career ambition to make money. On Friday evening, I did not go out and party. I did not want to socialize. I had a monumental decision to make as to whether I should trust God in Jesus with my life or not. I felt that this decision would alter my life, and yet I did not want to surrender my ego to anyone. Still, I knew in my spirit that it was all or nothing. I was sick of the spiritual struggle, so I got down on my knees on the floor of my dorm room on the third story of Hoekje Hall, Kalamazoo, Michigan, and I prayed in complete sincerity: "Jesus, if you are the God you claim to be in the bible, I would like to know you in a personal way. But I cannot follow a dead God. If you reveal yourself to me, I will follow you all the days of my life, but you must be real to me!"

It was an audacious and bold prayer. I was tired of playing religious games. I wanted to know the truth. If it was Jesus, then I would become a disciple, but if not, I would study Buddhism or some other religion. I went to bed that Friday night feeling nothing. The next morning, I awoke feeling strange. It was a good, strange feeling of freedom and joy. I was happy and at peace. The anger and darkness that I lived with constantly was gone.

I looked out the window of my room and felt like I was seeing the world as a new creation. I was experiencing a new spiritual birth. I did not read the bible; I did not talk to anyone; I did not do any righteous deed; I did not go to church or confess my sins. But I was changed. I was "born from above" by the Holy Spirit sent by Jesus and the Father. I walked around campus for three days on a natural high. My roommates thought the LSD was causing me to have flashbacks, but I was not using drugs anymore. A week later, I would buy a New American Standard Bible, and I would read St. Paul's letter to the Ephesians 5:18 describing the "Spirit-filled life":

> "Do not be drunken with wine for that is a waste, but be filled with the Spirit, speaking to each other with Psalms and hymns and spiritual songs, singing and making melody in your heart to the Lord."

A curious thing happened to me after my surrender to Jesus. I began to understand my childhood dreams of the Kingdom in the North. God, through the Holy Spirit, was calling me as a child to follow him. The Lord of the realm was Jesus, and the wind that constantly blew was the Holy Spirit. The faceless God to whom as a child I was doing homage was the Father God. It was a dream of heaven and the Trinity or Godhead, the three in one. The banners were God's protection over me and in me. The Ruach or wind of the Holy Spirit is the same wind that fell on the disciples in Acts 2:1-4 as a might rushing wind (Gk. Bia).

Prayer also changed. It became experiential. God's presence filled the room when I prayed. There was great joy and jubilation and a Presence that would make me feel that I was in my dream country. All of this happened prior to me reading or studying the Bible for myself. I was on the verge of my own mystical experiences and raptures with God. In college at Seattle Pacific University in 1972-75, I began to encounter other Christians who had radical conversions. In philosophy class, I read Blaise Pascal's Pensees. This is what the seventeenth century mathematician and philosopher sewed inside the hem of his coat on Nov. 23, 1654:

———

"The year of grace 1654. "Night Fire"
Monday, 23, November, feast of Saint Clement, Pope and martyr, and of others in martyrology, eve of St. Chrysogonus, Martyr and others. From about half past ten in the evening until half past midnight.

Fire

"God of Abraham, God of Isaac, God of Jacob, not of philosophers and scholars,
Certainty, certainty, heartfelt, joy, peace.
God of Jesus Christ.
God of Jesus Christ.
My God and your God. 'Thy God shall be my God.'
The world forgotten, and everything except God.
He can only be found by the ways taught in the Gospels.
Greatness of the human soul.
'O righteous Father, the world had not known thee, but I have known thee.'
Joy, joy, joy, tears of joy.
I have cut myself off from him.
They have forsaken me, the fountain of living waters.
'My God wilt thou forsake me?'
Let me not be cut off from him.
'And this eternal life, that they might know thee, the only

true God, and Jesus Christ whom thou hast sent.'
Jesus Christ. Jesus Christ."[4]

---

[4] *Pascal Pensees,* "The Memorial," trans. A.J. Krailsheimer (Baltimore: Penguin Books, 1966), 309-310.

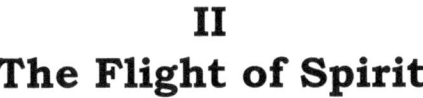

II
The Flight of Spirit

"Faith is the marriage of God and the soul."
St. John of the Cross

Finally, the Thanksgiving and Christmas holidays came in November and December of 1971. I came home with great joy and peace. I told my mother what had happened, and a surprised look came to her face. Thelma said, "I am happy for you." I had expected the golden ring to be put on my finger and a party thrown in my honor as in the parable of the Prodigal Son. My mother did not know what to think about my conversion. Her plan was for me to be the lawyer of the family, not a "Jesus' freak." I was surprised at the lack of enthusiasm that my family showed to me, and I felt like an orphan once again. Likewise, neither my high school friends nor college roommates understood my radical conversion to Jesus Christ. I was alone again…but not for long. I began to have mystical experiences in prayer.

Rufus Jones, the great Christian mystic and professor at Haverford College, wrote a book about his experiences with God, *Testimony of the Soul*, in which he defines a mystical experience with God as "the direct, immediate, transcending and unitive experience of God." As a baby Christian supposedly on a milk formula, I was suddenly given filet mignon by the Holy Spirit.

At 11:30 p.m., while praying on my bed, with my brother Jim sleeping in the bunk above me, I began to hear a roar like a jet passing over the house. The noise grew louder and louder. I continued to pray mentally with great joy and praise to the Father God as was my custom. I was drunk in the wine of the Holy Spirit and overflowing. Suddenly my entire body felt afire, as though tiny pinpricks were all over me. The roar became deafening, and I thought I was dying. I kept praying mentally, and my words were scattered all around like birdshot from a shotgun. I began to feel a sensation of speed as my soul seemed to be leaving my body or perhaps traveling somewhere at "warp speed." I left time and space, day and night, and was caught up by God into His Presence. I did not open my eyes, and I saw no images, no light, no darkness, just His Presence. It had nothing to do with subject or object. It was beyond empiricism and science. I was one with God who is love, and I was bathed in *agape*-love.

I was in the Spirit for about 30 minutes. When I returned to my physical body, I lay shaking for another 30 minutes. I could not comprehend what had happened to me. I had never heard of such a thing happening. I arose from my bed and typed up the experience so that I would have a record of it, which I still have today.

After the holiday, which was truly a Thanks-Giving to God, I talked to a mature Christian who was the campus director of Campus Crusade for Christ at WMU. Glen Matt listened to my prayer experience and said, "God chose to speak to you in this manner so you could understand it coming from your psychedelic experiences." That sounded reasonable to me but also very strange because the mystical experience in prayer was nothing like an LSD trip. Once one is on that hallucinogen, one is on it for seven to eight hours, and it is entirely a visual experience of colors, sounds, and sensations. My experience was non subject-object and apart from time and space.

I continued to go to the Campus Crusade meetings, and I also studied with Glen at his apartment on Friday evenings with a few other college students. Glen was a mentor to me and helped me learn Christian doctrine. I also attended church with him at a Dutch Reformed Church. Another person that helped me mature in Christ was a beautiful woman named Susan who was my first Christian girlfriend. Susan had dark hair, hazel eyes, and legs like a dancer, which she was. She was also very intelligent and had been involved with Youth for Christ in high school. It was through Susan's influence that I began to read Francis Schaeffer's book, *The God Who is There*. That book explained to me what the college professors were doing in my classes and why their philosophy of random chance and Skinner's behavioral modification theory left God out of the picture. The professors lived in a "closed universe" where God does not enter and there are no miracles, angels, demons, heaven, or hell.

Fall semester ended with Christmas break. Thank God! I was home again to enjoy mom's cinnamon rolls, turkey, rice pudding, and mincemeat pies. Ah! The delight of such smells and aromas wafting about our little house tucked between snowbanks and sugar maple trees! My house and its rural setting were right out of the "swinging on birches" poem of Robert Frost:

> *"I'd like to go by climbing a birch tree,*
> *And climb black branches up a*
> *snow-white trunk*
> *Toward heaven, till the tree*
> *could bear no more,*
> *But dipped its top and set me down again.*
> *That would be good both going*
> *and coming back.*
> *One could do worse than be a swinger of birches."[1]*

On Christmas Eve, I retired to my lower bunk bed and listened to the mice scurry about in the heating vents of our wood shake house. Even the mice sought warmth when it was below freezing all winter long. Remembering my previous encounter with the roar and leaving my body while caught up in the Spirit in Love, I began to pray with great exuberance. Again, I started to hear the sound of a jet engine far away. I prayed mentally, and soon the roar was all around me like the sound of Niagara Falls and a locomotive all at once. The fire fell again, and it was a "sweet burn" as St. John of the Cross called it in Living Flame of Love. I was out of time and space once again, but this time I felt no fear or anxiety, only bliss and unspeakable joy. Again, I was in his Presence and felt the Love that courses through all the cosmos and "holds all things together in him."[2]

Years later, in seminary, while taking a course with Fr. Michael Buckley, I read St. John of the Cross. I also read the spiritual classic

---

[1] Robert Frost, *Mountain Interval*, "Birches."

[2] 2 Col. 1:15 ESV.

The Interior Castle, written by Saint Teresa of Avila in 1577 at her Carmelite monastery in Spain. Teresa described my experience as the soul entering the sixth castle in the consecration experience:

" ... Well, now, to return to this quick rapture of the spirit. It is such that the spirit truly seems to go forth from the body. On the other hand, it is clear that this person is not dead; at least, he cannot say whether for some moments he was in the body or not. It seems to him that he was entirely in another region different from this in which we live, where there is shown another light so different from earth's light that if he were to spend his whole life trying to imagine that light, along with other things, he would be unable to do so ... whether all this takes place in the body or not, I wouldn't know; at least I wouldn't swear that the soul is in the body or that the body is without the soul.... What is true is that with the speed of a ball shot from an arquebus, when fire is applied, an interior flight is experienced. I don't know what else to call it."[3]

After I returned to WMU in January of 1971, I thought that it might be interesting to take a religion class since I was now a Christian. Dr. Lawson, a professor from South Africa, taught the class. He was an expert on African religions and animism, which is the belief that "inanimate objects and natural phenomena possess a personal life or soul."[4] He was not a Christian but had a seminary degree and a PhD. He spoke several languages and was quite brilliant. Students took his classes to argue with him. He had a reputation as a brilliant orator and debater, rather like St. Augustine before his conversion to Christianity. I did not know that Dr. Lawson bragged in class, "I can teach any course in the university, and if I don't know the material, I could fake it and nobody would know the difference!"

In my naiveté, I told the professor that I had become a "born again Christian," and that I was eager to take his class. The next day in the

---

[3] Teresa of Avilla, *The Interior Castle,*, Trans. Kiernan Kavanaugh and Otilio Rodriguez (New York: Paulist Press, 1979) 135-136

[4] *Webster's Collegiate Dictionary*, 28.

religion class, Dr. Lawson referred to me as a "Christian" in a rather snide fashion. I replied, "Yes, I am a Christian and happy to be saved." That statement opened the floodgates, and the professor and I had an hour-long debate over Jesus and the validity of the inspired scriptures. Please remember, I had been a believer for only two months, and I had read only the four gospels. I did not know form criticism or exegetical methods of scripture study or any hermeneutics (how to measure or study the Bible). I was a complete novice, and Dr. Lawson was the master of rhetoric.

Despite my limited knowledge of the Bible, I had something much better. I had the Holy Spirit of God living in my temple bringing to memory all that the Word taught. So, I opened my mouth and out came the words of the Comforter, the Paraclete of God (one who stands alongside). I gave a beautiful account of my conversion to Christ by praying a simple, sincere prayer to Jesus. Despite all the examples of the inconsistencies or errors in the Bible that the professor pointed out, he could not shake me from my experience of knowing the Personal, Living God. Not one other person spoke in the class for the entire period. After the class ended, Dr. Lawson remained to speak with me while the vultures gathered to attack me. The professor said to me, "You are wasting your time here at the university. You should be out in the world proclaiming your message." He was being congratulatory. He never spoke to lowly students after the instructional period.

The other students, many of whom were religion majors, were very angry, reminding me of the Pharisees of Jesus' time. They said, "You cannot know that your sins are forgiven!" "Yes, I can know, because I have been cleansed by the blood of Jesus," I replied. They were all in a huff, as though I had committed an unforgivable heresy, I walked out of the classroom feeling battered and bruised, but as I stepped out into the frigid winter air, the voice of God spoke to me very clearly from scripture: "Everyone who acknowledges me before men, I also will acknowledge before my Father who is in heaven, but whoever denies me before men, I also will deny before my Father who is in heaven."[5]

---

[5] Matt. 10:32 ESV.

Jesus said that when you are brought before the courts to give witness to your faith, the Holy Spirit will bring back to your memory the words to say. That is exactly what happened to me in my debate with Dr. Lawson and the hostile students. I lifted my head up and walked back to my dorm as gentle snowflakes began to fall from the sky, and I praised God "from whom all blessings flow." The name of Jesus is a mighty sword. Even as a young man and inexperienced Christian, I had the armor of God and the breastplate of righteousness that is YHWH TSIDKENU, "the Lord our righteousness."[6]

It began to dawn on me that I was not alone in this universe fending for myself as my humanistic professors proclaimed. I was a child of the King, and Jesus sent his angels to watch over me and protect me. I had begun to read the Psalms, the songbook of the bible, as part of my daily devotions. I especially enjoyed Psalm 91:11, 14-16, because it pertains to our deliverance from evil.

> "For he will command his angels   concerning you
> To guard you in all your ways ...
> Because he holds fast to me in love,
> I will deliver him;
> When he calls to me,
> I will answer him;
> I will be with him in trouble;
> I will rescue him and honor him with long life
> I will satisfy him
> And show him my salvation."

---

[6] Jer. 23:5-6 ESV.

III
Higher Education and the Football Angel

"Before Thee in humility, with Thee in faith,
in Thee in peace." (Dag Hammarskold)

For my junior year of college, I transferred to Seattle Pacific College in Seattle, Washington. I had asked my mother to send me some brochures of Christian colleges. Of all the schools, Seattle Pacific University stood out. I did not know a soul in Seattle. I had never been there. I liked the fact that Seattle did not get much snow. Puget Sound was beautiful in the shadows of the Cascade Mountains, and a large volcano about 80 miles north, Mt. Rainier, was snow-capped throughout the year. On a clear day, one could see the snow blowing on its peak. I took a giant leap of faith.

I came to this place trusting in the Lord to lead me. I desired to study biblical literature and philosophy. Philosophy was my favorite subject because I was blessed to study with Dr. Walter Johnson. His favorite saying was, "Think about this for ten or fifteen years!" This exceptional teacher was the first to tell me to study at the "Acropolis of schools," the Graduate Theological Union of Berkeley, California.

The other gift of providence from the Lord was meeting a beautiful coed named Jane Lust from Walnut Creek, California. Jane was an English major and wanted to be a teacher. We were engaged two years later, and after we graduated from SPU, we were married on August 24, 1974.

On one beautiful autumn day, my roommates and I drove from Seattle to Eugene, Oregon, to watch a football game between the Oregon Ducks and the Washington Huskies. The Bolin brothers, Jimmy, Dan, and Paul owned a Ford Pinto, a four-cylinder, low horsepower vehicle that could not climb some of the hills in Seattle. Its only redeeming feature was its good gas mileage. To break up the six-hour drive, we stopped in North Portland at the Bolin's family home. We got a home cooked meal and spent the night. The journey from there to Eugene was a three-hour drive on 1-5 South. For once it was not raining, and the good weather prevailed.

Once at the stadium, Jimmy informed us he had an extra ticket that we needed to sell for gas money to get home. I looked at my best friend, Dan Benson, the son of a Swedish chicken farmer from Kent, Washington, and we laughed out loud. Both teams were mediocre in 1972 before coach Don James made the University of Washington into a powerhouse team. The stadium was only half full, so they were giving away tickets. We had arrived an hour early to allow time to sell the ticket, but to no avail. To make matters worse, our ticket was a student ticket in the end zone. We were in a desperate situation. None of us owned credit cards, and we had no cash. We were carefree college students out on an adventure.

Since I was the dorm chaplain, I said to the boys, "Let's go over by the fence and pray and ask the Lord to help us sell the ticket." I knew we would not be able to sell it using our own ingenuity. We walked 25 yards away from the nearest person, got into a huddle, held hands, and prayed. I was the last to pray. I held the ticket in my closed left hand. Before I ended my prayer, a man walked up to me and said, "I'd like to buy that ticket that you have in your hand." I was so shocked that I could not speak. "Well," he said, "How much is it?" How could he even see the ticket? I had it clenched in my hand. I looked at the ticket and said, "It is five dollars."

The man was of average height and weight and looked like an Oregon farmer. He wore a brown, weathered jacket and work pants and old leather shoes. He opened his well-used brown billfold and counted out five crumpled dollar bills. I held out my hand, and he counted them off to me, "one, two, three, four, five." I thought to myself, "This guy thinks I am a school child or something." We all said, "Thanks, mister," and ran into the stadium as the game was about to begin.

Since our five seats were together, I took the aisle seat, and the stranger took the seat across the aisle from me, midway up in the end zone of the Oregon Ducks' side. Each of us looked over and studied the man from time to time throughout the game. I was especially interested in him because I thought he might be an angel in disguise. He obviously was not a football fan! All during the game, he stared into the sky and surveyed the stadium. He seemed very bored, even though it turned out to be a very exciting football game.

With two minutes left in the fourth quarter, the Huskies drove the ball down the field to the Ducks 20-yard line. The Washington team broke a 10-10 tie, and the Huskies won the game. During this most exciting part of the game, the mysterious man disappeared. It was so strange, even peculiar. The man did not walk past me up the aisle. I would have seen him leave. He just vanished. We discussed the stranger at length on our drive home.

We reached an easy consensus: The man dressed like an Oregon farmer was in reality an angel sent from God to help us. Over the years, when we would talk on the phone or have vacation visits, the five of us sometimes talk about the angel. Why would God the Father send an angel to our rescue over a silly football game? Simply because Jesus loves us, and we are a part of the family of God. We are a blood-covenant family, and though we are created lower than the angels, someday we will rule over them in God's providence. The writer of Hebrews reminds us that "some have entertained angels unawares."[1]

"Since therefore the children share in flesh and blood, he himself likewise partook of the same things, that through death he might destroy the one who has the power of death, that is the devil, and deliver all those who through fear of death were subject to lifelong slavery. For surely it is not angels that he helps, but he helps the offspring of Abraham. Therefore, he had to be made like his brothers in every respect, so that he might become a merciful and faithful high priest in the service of God, to make propitiation for the sins of the people. For because he himself has suffered when tempted, he is able to help those who are being tempted."[2]

---

[1] Heb. 13:2 ESV
[2] Heb. 2:14-18.

IV
Elitch Gardens, 1944

"No weapon that is fashioned against you shall succeed and you shall confute every tongue that rises against you in judgment. This is the heritage of the servants of the Lord." (Isaiah 54:17 ESV)

During World War II, my mother dropped out of college at the University of Nebraska and moved to Denver, Colorado, to work at the Denver Drive Department Store. My grandmother, Sadie Zoppelli, was not happy about Thelma's decision. Thelma was an attractive Swedish-German girl with long, chestnut brown hair and hazel eyes. She rode horses on her parents' ranch and milked Holstein cows to help her family through the depression years of the 1930s. Thelma's favorite was a quarter horse named Ginger Boy. But as the war devastated Europe, she became a serious working woman in the big city of Denver. She decided to cut her hair short.

Soldiers were stationed in Denver in support of the troops overseas. My mother, only 20 years old, went out on dates with the young soldiers who were her age also. The most popular place for entertainment at that time was Elitch Gardens, an amusement park with rides and dance halls and restaurants. Lawrence Welk, Tommy Dorsey, and Glen Miller's big bands played there. The amusement park had orchards and gardens when it was purchased by Mr. Elitch and his wife in 1891. Later it became more of an amusement park with rides like the "Tunnel of Love."

Thelma loved stylish hats that she got using her employee discount from the Denver Drive. With a smart-looking hat and a date with a handsome soldier, she went to Elitch Gardens for a fun night out on the town. The Tunnel of Love was popular among dating couples for obvious reasons. She stood in line with her date for 30 minutes. When they were next in line, Thelma suddenly felt an existential dread of this ride. More than a foreboding, it was a feeling of doom and death. She told the soldier that she could not go on the ride despite waiting a long time in line. Her date suggested that they have a Coke and sit down for a while. So, they sat down and started talking about their lives and future plans. A few minutes into their conversation, they smelled smoke and heard shouts coming from the ride that they had been next in line to take. To their great horror, they saw the Tunnel of Love go up in flames. The old wooden tunnel became an inferno, and six people died, including the couple who had taken their place.

This tragedy occurred on July 16, 1944. The newspaper account is as follows:

"Fire erupted in the old Tunnel of Love, trapping and burning six screaming patrons alive. The old wooden tunnel turned into a raging inferno by the time firemen arrived. It was out of control within minutes. As thick black smoke billowed to a height of over 150 feet in the air, the fire engines were delayed by a locked gate. Since no one knew what caused it, a coroner's inquest was held. It blamed the age of the attraction, ignorance, neglect, and carelessness. The six patrons died of smoke inhalation."[1]

My mother told me this story about six years ago, before she began to lose her memory from Alzheimer's Disease. As she lay dying at the age of 91, I researched this event on the computer, because my brother Jim was skeptical that it had happened. We all sat down and read the account together as a family. We were astounded by the story.

The soldier with Thelma that day was very shaken by the tragedy and told my mother, "I will never throw this ticket away because it reminds me of how close I came to death." As a soldier, he was especially aware of war and death. The young man must have thought my mother was very lucky or even psychic, but it was deeper than that. She was closely attuned to the world of the Spirit of God. Thelma grew up as a "dreamer of dreams" and had "second sight," like a prophet having a vision of the future.

When I gave the eulogy for Thelma Foresteen Zoppelli Lynch's memorial service in Grand Blanc, Michigan, I recounted my mother's

[1] <[*lostamusementparks.org/articles/elitchgardens.html*]>

unique gift of being able to see into the future with God's help through the Holy Spirit. My radical conversion to Christianity was a direct result of my mother's countless prayers for her "prodigal son." My mother named me after the Archangel Michael, the protector of Israel. She assured me that I had guardian angels watching over me and that I was predestined to be conformed to the image of God's Son, through Jesus Christ. When I entered San Francisco Theological Seminary in San Anselmo, California, Thelma told me of my baptism as a baby at the First Presbyterian Church in Flint., sp. She believed in the Apostle's Creed and these words from it: "I believe in the Holy Ghost; the holy catholic Church; the communion of saints; the forgiveness of sins; the resurrection of the body; and life everlasting."[2]

Thelma lived a consecrated life in the truest meaning of the word, "to make one's hands full of God and to be whole." Her constant, vigilant prayers were heard by God and answered. Thelma knew there is "no defense against Spirit led prayer." My mother was spared death in 1944 because of her mother's prayers and the will of God. My mother would say that "If you believe you are in Christ, you are elected," as stated in Second Helvetic Confession. While in seminary, I was required to read and know the Confessions and Creeds of the Church, which today most Christians seldom think about. The Second Helvetic Confession was written in Switzerland in 1566 by Heinrich Bullinger, a theologian and friend of John Calvin. It is the longest of the Confessions and most thorough from a reformed perspective. In section 5.060, Bullinger wrote the following about predestination:

"Let Christ, therefore, be the looking glass, in whom we may contemplate our predestination. We shall have a sufficiently clear and sure testimony that we are inscribed in the Book of Life if we have fellowship with Christ, and He is ours and we are His in true faith."[3]

My mother was laid to rest in a beautiful cemetery next to my father in Mt. Morris, Michigan, on September 9, 2015. It was a grey

---

[2] (The Book of Confession, United Presbyterian Church, section 2.3.) 473 Riverside Dr. New York, N.Y.

[3] Ibid, 5.060

and overcast day with the temperature in the low 50s. As I stood over the perfectly dug, rectangular grave and the casket perched over it like a harbinger of her true home in heaven with the angels and saints, I prayed one last prayer for her. I put roses on the shiny white casket about to be fouled by earth and stone and the worm of corruption. Thelma is not there, however, decaying in the grave. She is at her home with my father and his brother and the saints that have gone before her and, of course, with Jesus, her Lord and Savior.

In my eulogy at the memorial service, I told my family and the friends of my mother about a prophetic dream that I had in March of 2015, seven months before Thelma's death:

> "I awoke from a very vivid dream of my mother's death. My father Jeff and his brother Johnny came to me in the dream. They were young and handsome and robust. The two brothers were in their twenties and were smiling and very happy. They said to me, 'Thelma is with us, and you need not worry about her.' Jeff and Johnny were in heaven with all the saints, and Thelma was rejoicing with them!"

After the burial service, we drove to Frankenmuth, Michigan, to my mother's favorite restaurant, The Bavarian Inn, and had a celebration dinner with baked chicken and all the gourmet trimmings. Of course, the younger folks in our party of thirty ordered German beer, and we toasted Thelma Lynch in the tradition of an Irish wake. There was no dancing; everything was done in Presbyterian decorum of "decently and in order." It provided everyone a sense of closure after the long ordeal of Thelma's decline and death.

In typical Detroit fashion, there was a hot rod and muscle car show going on in the entire town. As we walked out of the restaurant in our suits and formal attire, muscle cars were revving their engines and super chargers. The drivers were showing off their cars to a parade of people standing along the curb. The air was full of carbon emissions and the smell of burning rubber. Yes, this was Michigan, the land of automobiles, factories, and beautiful landscapes of birch and pine forests, with the Great Lakes and white, mountainous sand dunes! I

was home to say one last goodbye to my sweet mother. For me, Thelma was like Monica, the mother of Augustine, who prayed him into the Kingdom of God.

V
The Fonz and Mount Diablo

"Angels are watching; they mark your path. They superintend the events of your life and protect the interest of the Lord God, always working to promote his plans and to bring his highest will for you." (Billy Graham)

In the spring of 1970, Jane and her best friend, Gretchen, were driving up the zigzag road to Mount Diablo State Park a few miles from their home in Walnut Creek, California. Jane and Gretchen were both seniors at Ygnacio Valley High School in Walnut Creek. It was Saturday. They wanted to relax from their studies out in nature.

Mount Diablo's two peaks are the remnant of an extinct volcano that overlooks the East Bay of San Francisco. On a clear day, one can see Mt. Hamilton to the south and several bridges spanning the bays. As one flies into the Bay Area, the two most prominent landmarks are the San Mateo Bridge and the twin peaks of Mount Diablo. The 4,000-foot mountain was named by the Spanish soldiers because of sightings of the devil there, and because an entire tribe of Native Americans had disappeared into the mountain as the Conquistadors were seeking to capture them. The natives considered the mountain to be holy and made pilgrimages there.

The day was sunny and warm, and the spring flowers dotted the mountainside. This tranquil scene was rudely interrupted by a swarm of motorcycle riders that cut the girls off and pulled in front of their car. Jane was scared and said, "Gun it, Gretchen. They are going to block us in." Instead, Gretchen slowed the car and stopped. The gang surrounded the car and was going to have some fun at the two young ladies' expense. Jane was thinking to herself, "We are in big trouble now." Other cars, full of families, not wanting to get involved, drove by without slowing down. Jane and Gretchen were unprepared for this. Their comfy lives in affluent Walnut Creek were about to be delivered a serious "wake up call." The leather-clad motorcycle club, with colors flying, opened the hood of the car and removed the distributor cap. It was becoming increasingly serious.

In California, during this same period of time, the film "Easy Rider" glamorized a lifestyle of rebellion, freedom from laws and "square people" who were not hip to this new-age, pagan way of thinking. The television series, "Happy Days," was very popular. Its anti-hero, "the Fonz," was not interested in schooling and always had attractive women around. He was a tough guy, wore a black leather jacket, and regularly slicked back his hair. He lived by his own rules. He was a cool dude.

Jane and Gretchen sat in their four-door sedan, feeling very scared and alone. They had no idea what the gang had planned, but it was certainly not a fun trip to the park. Suddenly, a man appeared from the hillside. He looked like "the Fonz." He wore blue jeans and a white T-shirt, and he even had slicked back hair. He wore no leathers, so they were sure he was not part of the gang. The Fonz took the distributor cap from the motorcyclists and reinstalled it in the car. Nobody in the gang said a word to him. The man told Jane and Gretchen, "Everything will be okay, girls. You can start your car and leave." The biker gang cleared a path for them, and the two girls drove up the road into the park. The Fonz disappeared as suddenly as he had appeared. Jane told me this after we were married. She believed the man was an angel sent by God in their time of distress. Strangely, the girls never spoke of the incident.

Both Jane and Gretchen attended churches. Gretchen was Episcopalian, and Jane was a member of the Evangelical Free Church. Signs and wonders were not a vital topic in either church. Episcopalians did not profess miracles, and one of their bishops, Bishop A. T. Robinson, was preaching the "death of God" in his famous book, Honest to God. Jane's church believed in the bible and miracles, but did not talk about them and had not seen many. They believed that the gifts of the Holy Spirit ended with the death of the last apostles of Christ. Jane never accepted this faulty theology; she longed for a supernatural God and signs and wonders. Her reasoning was straightforward: "Why follow a dead God?" If God is personal and dynamic as in the creation of the universe, time and space, angels and even devils, then he must be able to reveal himself in the person of Jesus. Otherwise, he is not worth following!

Around the time that Jane saw the angel of God, she was called out of her high school class to talk to a complete stranger. The gentleman was a recruiter from Seattle Pacific College in Seattle, Washington. Jane had not requested information from this Christian college, but she wanted to leave the Bay Area to attend college. Her parents would not allow her to apply to the University of California at Berkeley, because they thought it was too radical with all of the Vietnam War protests and the "Free Speech Movement."

Jane was impressed by the man's presentation about this Free Methodist College. She was considering majoring in English. She had been playing piano and taking lessons since the age of four. Even then, she had nearly perfect pitch and began playing on the piano the tunes that she heard on the radio. She convinced her parents to let her attend the college in the Pacific Northwest. This was a fortuitous event for both of us. I transferred to SPC from Western Michigan University in 1972, during my junior year. We met at a Campus Crusade for Christ meeting at SPC during my first year. In 1973, Jane wrote to me in a letter, "The first time I talked to you in October of 1971, I wrote to my mom and told her I was in love with this guy that just transferred from Michigan named Mike."

Both of us were guided to this college by the Holy Spirit. We were predestined to meet and eventually marry, contrary to my previously stated desires. I did not want to surrender my life to Christ because I wanted to be a lawyer and make a lot of money in international law and move to Europe and marry a beautiful European woman. God's plan, however, was this introduction to Jane, German-American, musically talented, intelligent, and beautiful.

The college became Seattle Pacific University in 1974. About 2,000 students lived on campus, and another 2,000 were commuters or graduate students. It was a holiness school, meaning that they ascribed to the teachings of John and Charles Wesley and the First Great Awakening in America. I wrote a paper on George Whitefield and his "field preaching" in America in the 1730s and 1740s. I felt that Wesley had a much better understanding than did John Calvin of the Holy Spirit and sanctification, becoming full of God and holy. Like me, Jane longed for the deeper life in the Spirit. While in high school, she attended a David Wilkerson rally at the Oakland Coliseum. She saw people throwing away their drugs, demons being cast out of people, signs and wonders, and people speaking and singing in tongues. (See Acts 2 in the New Testament.) Wilkerson was a prophet, famous for starting Teen Challenge.

After my conversion to Jesus Christ, the church that my parents attended had become fundamentalist, and they used the C.I. Scofield Study Bible. The church was a "Dispensationalist Church." They were more interested in the law of God than the grace of God. Since we were in the Church Age and not the Apostolic Age, they believed that the charismata, the gifts of the Holy Spirit, had ceased.

This dispensationalist movement was begun by the Plymouth Brethren in England in the 1800s and had spread to American from the Keswick prophetic bible conferences beginning in 1878. The conferences were held annually at Niagara-on-the-Lake in Ontario, Canada. John Nelson Darby and the Brethren emphasized that there were seven periods of history (dispensations), and that God worked only one way in each time period. Since we are currently in the Church Age, the previous dispensation of the apostles and prophets is over, and the bible has become the Holy Spirit for these believers. Therefore, they said, the more Bible one has, the more Holy Spirit one has. Darby also taught that every believer is sealed by the Holy Spirit for the day of redemption, but one is filled by the Holy Spirit for works, such as missions. The Christological center moved from "Jesus in us, the hope of glory," to the Spirit as our witness living in us passively. The result of this shift in theology was a disaster! Dr. Samuel J. Stoesz, in his important book, Sanctification, an Alliance Distinctive, summarizes these thoughts:

> "Thus, the dominant emphasis of the Higher Christian Life Movement was lost by default and not by overt opposition. As it evolved into the Keswick Movement and as Keswick was

increasingly influenced by dispensationalism, 'Christ Himself' was no longer emphasized. More and more sanctification was associated with the initial act of salvation. The carnal nature of the believer was by nature from earth and to be 'suppressed' by the Spirit in this dispensation of the church and of the Spirit. The shift from a Christological emphasis in sanctification to a pneumatological one associated with 'power for service' becomes prominent in Keswick and in mainstream American evangelicalism. This gave impetus to mainstream Pentecostalism."[1]

Both Jane and I had been taught this erroneous theology that had crept into the church. In our theology, however, we were spared this mistake of Evangelical Christianity in regard to dispensationalism by attending a Wesleyan college where sanctification remained Christ-centered, and our experiences in the Charismatic movement kept our focus on Christ as baptizer in the Spirit. Jane was attending a charismatic Presbyterian church on Queen Anne Hill near the college, and I was reading Dennis and Rita Bennett's book, Nine O'clock in the Morning. I began to pray in tongues (glossolalia).

Even for the Free Methodist college, the charismatic gifts were a bit much. All of our guest speakers were evangelicals, such as Dr. John Stott, Dr. Elton Trueblood, Tom Skinner, Vernon Grounds, and John Perkins, all of whom were involved in social action and biblical scholarship. They did not, however, speak of sanctification and the filling of the Spirit as a definite second experience. Stott wrote that the filling of the Spirit was by faith, and it equipped the saints to do the work of the Gospel. Dr. Stott also did not talk about the charismatic gifts of prophesy, word of knowledge, healing, tongues, or discernment of evil spirits. It was not part of either their experience or their doctrine.

It was not an accident that both Jane and I have had experiences with angels at a young age. In my family, I was taught that guardian angels are real and sent by Jesus to protect the elect and do warfare against evil spirits and demons. Jane's grandparents, the Krafts, were very devout, Spirit-led Christians and lived next door to Jane's family

[1] Samuel J. Stoesz, *Sanctification, an Alliance Distinctive* (Camp Hill: Camp Hill Christian Pub., 1992), 42-43.

in Walnut Creek. She was, in fact, so attached to her Nana Kraft's cooking that she turned down an invitation by me and my friends from SPC to go into San Francisco to see the sights with us. After we were married and I came to know the grandparents well, I realized what Godly people they were and how they prayed and walked with Christ. Jane's heritage was as rooted in Christianity as mine. Jane's mother Del and her father Lester were also devout and prayed every day for us. I am confident that at times they felt like my mother Thelma, that God was not hearing their prayers because we appeared to be in a constant "computer loop."

VI
Seminary or Cemetery

"A distinguished theological professor has said that the question ought to be put to every candidate for the ministry, 'Have you met God?' Yes, but we ought to go further than this …. 'Have you been baptized with the Holy Spirit?'" (R. A. Torrey, The Person and Work of the Holy Spirit)

After Jane and I were married, the reality of a major recession in the economy hit us in the face. We were young, naive, and deeply in love. Jane held the belief that "You do not marry a person that you can live with; you marry a person you cannot live without." Despite not having jobs or even a place to live, we were married in Jane's back yard by her uncle, the Rev. Vernon Kraft. Our best friends from SPC drove down to California from Seattle, and my brother Jim and sister Linda came from Michigan and North Carolina. Music for the wedding was provided by a classical guitarist and a pianist, and Jane's friend, Wendy, an opera singer, sang the prayer of St. Francis. It was a simple ceremony, yet very beautiful.

We both learned very rapidly that no matter how deeply in love a couple is, they must work to pay the bills. Silicon Valley had many jobs, but they were "high tech." We had humanities degrees. Jane's was in literature, and mine was in biblical studies and philosophy. So, we packed up what little we had and moved into a small, wooden, summer house with no insulation on the shores of Puget Sound in Des Moines, Washington. The camp was called Covenant Beach. Our best friends, Dan and Sig Benson, lived there with their two-year-old baby, Gretchen.

We all lived in community at the retreat center in little houses dotting the green, fern-laden hillside. Our pets roamed freely along the creek that ran into Puget Sound. Those pets were the huge, yellow Banana Slugs and Norwegian river rats that lived under the bridge leading to our shack. A large owl population ate the rats, much to our relief. During these days of unemployment, underemployment, and injuries, I had much time to read and meditate upon God. Jane and Dan commuted to work in Seattle every day while I rehabilitated from two knee surgeries and a torn Achilles tendon. I spent the first three years of our marriage in leg or ankle casts.

While this appeared to be a by-product of all my years playing sports in school, it was in actuality the spiritual experience of "purgation" and the "dark night of the soul." (From St. John of the Cross, 16th century)

To nurture my soul and spirit during this "long dark night," I read A. W. Tozer and the Catholic mystics, St. Teresa, St. John of the Cross, and Meister Eckhart (14th century German mystic). I continued to read the sermons of Eckhart, whom many scholars credit with being the forerunner of the reformation of the church by Luther and Calvin. In his sermon, "God laughs and plays," Eckhart, quoting Isaiah 49:13 and John 8:12, wrote this:

> "Be as sure of it as you are that God lives: at the least good deeds, the least bit of good will, or the least of good desires, all the saints in heaven and on earth rejoice, and together with the angels, their joy is such that all the joy in the world cannot be compared to it. The more exalted a saint is, the greater his joy; but the joy of them all put together amounts to as little as a bean when compared to the joy of God over good deeds. For truly, God plays and laughs in good deeds, whereas all other deeds, which do not make for the glory of God, are like ashes before Him."[1]

In my solitude in the Pacific Northwest marine climate, I had many days and nights to ponder my life and calling in Christ. I went through days, weeks, and months when the heavens were silent as a bronze dome. In these days of silence, I was reduced to simplicity. Jane thought we were cursed for the sins of our past since nothing seemed to work out for us. Nobody could give us solace. We felt "rejected and despised of men." Then, in the middle of our "dark night," a little light broke through. During the gloomy Seattle winter, I read a sermon by Meister Eckhart written before 1328 that gave me hope:

---

[1] Meister Eckhart, *Meister Eckhart*, trans. Raymond B. Blakney (New York: Harper and Row, 1941) 143.

"When you are about to begin a new life or work, go to God and ask with all your might and devotion that He will make it turn out for the best, as it seems most agreeable and fitting to Him and be sure you are not thinking of your own advantage but only of God's dearest will and nothing else. Then whatever God brings about, take it as direct from Him--the best as He sees it--and be completely satisfied!"[2]

Meister Eckhart's advice was wise and timely for me. I wrote in the margin of the text the date, January 9, 1976. During this time period, I became a Presbyterian youth minister intern at The Wedgwood Presbyterian Church in Seattle. The Rev. Budge Gere had advertised the position on a job board at SPC. Jane was finishing her teaching credential at the college, saw the job listing, and gave it to me. I was excited about the position and applied for it. Budge had worked at the University Church in Ann Arbor, Michigan, and knew the minister that baptized me as an infant, Rev. Molineaux. I had a Presbyterian background, at least through my parents, so he hired me. It was only thirty hours a week with no benefits, but it was a job in ministry.

We moved from our retreat center on Puget Sound to an equally beautiful place amid Douglas Fir trees overlooking Lake Washington in North Seattle. We rented a small mother-in-law apartment from the music director of the church. Jane was doing student teaching at a large urban high school in White Center in West Seattle. After I had served only ten months at the Wedgwood Church, the elders decided to end my position as a paid staff member. The church was on a tight budget, and they decided they could save money by having lay people volunteer in the youth program. The church had fired their previous senior minister and youth worker, and they were still trying to find their way. Rev. Gere suggested that I apply to San Francisco Theological Seminary. He was the second person to suggest that school to me. The first was my philosophy professor, Dr. Walter Johnson.

Jane and I had zero cash reserves. My mother had even paid for Jane to get her teaching credential. I was driving around in a blue Opel that my mother had given me as a graduation present. We were as poor

2 *Ibid.*, "How to follow after God and some good ways to do it," 34.

as church mice! On top of that, I had a student loan to pay back from my fifth year in college at SPC. It was only $1,000but to us, at that time, it was a lot of money. My car had cost$1,800.

Nevertheless, Jane was very excited about moving to Marin County, north of the Golden Gate Bridge, one of the wealthiest and most beautiful counties in the country. It was called "fabulous Marin County!" The seminary was part of a consortium of schools called the GTU. Graduate Theological Union was located in the hills above UC Berkeley.

Since we had no money in our banking account, the dean of students offered me a full grant for tuition. I was shocked! I had never before been given any money for education. Jane's grandfather, Ed Kraft, gave me money for books as long as I was in seminary. I saw this as the hand of God in my life and took it as a sign that we were on the right path. Jane was one of the few wives that worked. There were not many jobs in the area. John Irvine, the dean of students, told Jane that no seminary wife had received work as a teacher in ten years. Jane found work at Santa Barbara Savings and Loan on San Anselmo Avenue, two blocks from the school. We were blessed with her job and the health benefits it provided. The seminary was a sister school to Princeton Theological Seminary, and the professors were all Ivy League graduates of Yale, Harvard, or Princeton. I would find out later that those credentials did not make one a man or woman of God.

I loved my courses at the GTU in Berkeley, where I studied with Jesuits and Dominicans primarily, and I was able to pursue my love for biblical studies, Christian mysticism, and philosophy. I took my required core classes at the Presbyterian Seminary. Some of the Presbyterian professors challenged me regarding my evangelical theology. I did not swallow verbatim all the latest fads and critical systems that they created. I still believed that the bible was the written inspired Word of God (theopnuestas-God breathed). I was like a theological dinosaur to most of the elitist PhD's from Yale and Harvard.

One professor in particular gave me a hard time for rejecting the documentary hypothesis view of Julius Wellhausen, which stated that the Pentateuch (first five books of the bible) was written not by

Moses but by four editors known as Jahwist, Elohimist, Priestly, and Deuteronomist. They were referred to as JEPD. This way of exegeting the Bible destroyed the flow and continuity of the Scripture by cutting and pasting the bible together using the various names for God in Hebrew. Moses was given one sentence as the original author in the Pentateuch. I thought that this hypothesis, which was universally accepted in academic theological scholarship, was absurd and heretical.

On February 26,1978, I submitted my 19-page paper with 47 footnotes to Professor Coote. The title of my paper was "A Revelational Approach to the Scriptures as Applied to Deuteronomy." The professor was irate with my evangelical approach to the interpretation of Deuteronomy. He wrote on every page, criticizing all my presuppositions and exegesis of the book. It is true that I did not write a concise six-page exegesis on the Shemah or song of Moses using the method of JEPD. What I wrote was a counterproposal to biblical scholarship of Deuteronomy using the best of evangelical scholarship. Dr. Coote gave me an "Inc." He refused to grade the paper and wrote this statement on it:

"I can't understand. I can see you are dissatisfied with what you see as the presupposition of critical study, and that you want to substitute 'a priori suppositions.' But where do they come from, and what affect do they have on interpretation of scripture? How would your understanding of the original intent of Dt. differ from critics? Why didn't you just do what your title suggests: explain your revelational approach' and apply it to Dt.? Leave out all the quotes. Be clear. Work on coherence. Shorten it. I think by being negative sounding you have over-aroused the negative in me, Mike! But that is better than just dismissing this paper as a muddle. You must take these criticisms seriously and work on communicating your ideas and feelings more clearly!"

On my first day in seminary, as all of us sat together in orientation, this same professor, Dr. Coote, gave us a talk on the bible. I will never forget what he said about it. He hemmed and hawed and said, "The bible, the bible, what can I say about this ancient book?" The professor was emotional and profoundly moved by the Bible, which he read in

Hebrew only. But ultimately, he could not say what it is "God breathed by men of old being carried along by the Holy Spirit." The esteemed professor of the Hebrew department said nothing of consequence as to the written Word of God. He believed it was written by various authors and edited by fallible men.

The author of Hebrews, however, clearly knew and expressed what the bible is about: "For the Word of God is living and active, sharper than any two-edged sword, piercing to the division of soul and spirit, of joints and of marrow, and discerning the thoughts and intentions of the heart. And no creature is hidden from his sight, but all are naked and exposed to the eyes of him to whom we must give account."[3]

For me, the three years I spent at SFTS were as sterile and lifeless as a cemetery. Everything was done decently and in order, but it had the fragrance of death. "The Lord is the Spirit, and wherever the Spirit is, there is life." But if the Spirit is absent or grieved, then the corollary is true: there is the" dust of death."

The one bright spot in this "theological muddle" was Dr. Robert A. Pitman and the First Presbyterian Church of San Mateo. We began attending when Gary Cox, a fellow classmate and member of the church, invited us. Located on 25th and Hacienda Drive, the church had just 1,000 members. It was evangelical in theology, had a large choir both adult and youth, and the sermons were biblical and practical. The Holy Spirit was in this place. Jane and I fell in love with it!

The seminary required a third year in the field for Master of Divinity candidates. I chose the San Mateo church under Rev. Bob Pitman's supervision. I had liked Bob and his wife Marilyn immediately. They were kindred spirits. Jane and I rented an apartment in Belmont, just a few miles south of the church. The apartment was at the top of a large hill that overlooked a canyon that went down to Crooked Dog Lake where I would walk, meditate, and pray. Jane found a job in a bank because she had experience in the field. I commuted to the San Anselmo campus on Mondays for class. The rest of my time was spent at the church where I had been put in charge of the junior high ministry. As an intern minister, I was at the low rung of the ladder in

[3] Heb. 4:12-13.

the Presbyterian power structure. Nevertheless, I enjoyed the members that I recruited to help. The parents were also very involved in the church and in the lives of their teenagers.

Lance and Pam Vining were the music ministers. Pam was an accomplished pianist from an east coast conservatory of music, and Lance had a trained operatic soprano voice. Jane and I loved hearing the classical music as well as the contemporary praise music. One day at church, Lance asked me to lead a short devotional bible study before his teen choir, The Spirit Spreaders, sang in their Sunday afternoon rehearsals. I gladly agreed, since I knew many of the young people in the choir. I had enjoyed reading the Christian Missionary and Alliance writer A.W. Tozer, so I decided to read a few portions from his booklet, Keys to the Deeper Life. The topic was "The Filling of the Holy Spirit for the Christian."

The youth choir was large. Thirty young people were in attendance on this particular Sunday. We sat in the back of the long, narrow, cathedral-like church with the beautiful stained-glass windows reflecting the spring sunshine. The senior pastor, Bob Pitman, and his wife Marilyn were in the front of the church doing something unrelated to the choir. First, we prayed. Then I began to share four points from the Tozer booklet on how to be filled with the Holy Spirit. My premise, like Dwight Moody's at the turn of the twentieth century, was that Christians need to be filled with the Holy Spirit because we "leak!" Our old carnal nature wants to direct our lives. Tozer's booklet provided four steps with accompanying Scriptures on how to achieve this Spirit-filling process.

1. Entire surrender of your life to Jesus (Rom. 12:1-2; Rom. 8:11-17)
2. Ask the Spirit to come upon you! (Luke 11:9-13)
3. Obey God! Acts 5:32; Acts 10:44-48; Gal. 3:2-3)
4. Believe in Jesus and His Word (Mark 16:17; Gal. 3:22; James 1:16

I had not spoken more than ten minutes when the fire from heaven fell upon us all, teens and adults. It was like Pentecost, but inside a mainline Presbyterian church. The students began to weep and confess their sins, all done spontaneously. Daryl Wilson began to prophesy, and others were speaking in tongues (unknown languages) and praising God in the Spirit. The young people laid hands on each other and prayed for healing. The Holy Spirit had fallen upon everyone there without warning. God was in charge of the choir. Unspeakable joy and praise of Jesus echoed off the tall, steep ceiling of the sanctuary. The pastor and his wife sat in the front of the church and went along with the flow of the Holy Spirit. There was no human leader, only the Wind of God, the Holy Spirit! This worship and praise continued for three hours. No music was practiced that day. The Spirit Spreaders choir would never be the same.

Rev. Pitman began to receive calls from angry parents almost immediately. Some parents were upset that there had been no music practice, only prayer and praise for three hours. At this time in the life of the church, 1979-1985, about a quarter of the church was charismatic. To meet the need for Spirit-filled worship, the church held a Friday night prayer and praise group that grew to about 100 people. Drs. Jeanne and Paul Linquist and Don and Audrey Wilson were among its early leaders. Jane and I were involved with the leadership of this Friday evening group as well. There were, however, many Christians in the congregation that thought it was too emotional and not reformed in theology. John Calvin had taught that the gifts of the Spirit that the Anabaptists in Germany and Switzerland were practicing were not necessary. The session, the ruling body in the Presbyterian Church, passed a rule that an elder had to be present on Sunday afternoons for the Spirit Spreaders choir rehearsals. Jane and I were shocked, as were Lance and Pam Vining. I believe this rule quenched the fire of the Holy Spirit in the church.

Nevertheless, Rev. Pitman asked me to accompany him to Texas and Colorado for the Spirit Spreaders choir trip in the summer. The young people performed a musical of contemporary praise music. Many people in the churches were blessed. The choir members lives were changed also. Some became ministers and missionaries, and all of them learned what it means to "worship in the Spirit and truth!" The Wilsons became our good friends, and their son Daryl went on to attend Oral Roberts University and then Fuller Seminary. Today he is a Presbyterian minister to two yoked churches in Idaho.

In the summer of 1980, which was my last year in seminary, I had not yet received a call to a Presbyterian Church, despite many interviews and trips to various congregations. I was quite depressed, but not as much as Jane. She had worked for three years in boring bank jobs so we could survive economically. I was the only one in my class of forty men and women who had not received a job offer. So when the Wilson's offered me a week at a Christian camp called CFO, I took it. This unique camp was started by Glen Clark in the 1930s. The acronym stood for Camp Farthest Out. The camp combined physical exercise with worship and speakers who were charismatic and prophetic in their teaching. I was given a cabin with no roof among the tall Ponderosa pines. It was like a hermitage where I could be alone, pray, and meditate on God's word and hopefully receive direction for my life. I felt like the Trappist monk, Thomas Merton, alone in his hut in the Kentucky woods.

Two prophets entered my life at the camp. They were Dick and Judy French from Parsons, Kansas. They were Midwesterners with a deep prayer life and many gifts of the Holy Spirit. They were wise, biblically grounded, and walked in the power of the Holy Spirit. These two prophets were the ones who told me, "God's supply depots are scattered along the road of obedience." (Tommy Tyson)

When the week-long camp had ended, the Wilson's had a party at their house in Foster City for those people who wanted to talk with Dick and Judy French. Jane was not in a party mood, but she came with me because I insisted that she meet the Frenches. We were both angry and bewildered because I could not find a job as a licensed Presbyterian minister. At the party, Jane asked Dick and Judy to pray for us. Judy said to us, "Kneel down and we will lay hands on you for God's blessing." We both knelt before the prophets, and many people prayed for us. A sixteen-year-old cousin of the Wilson's had a vision, and Van described it as follows: "I see a round wooden door with bars on it. There is a pile of rocks piled up around the door. The rocks are crying out, "We want God. We want God.""

VII
The Irish Channel

"Dear Lord, teach me the way to poverty. It is so clear that possessions lead to many false worries and that these worries prevent me from paying attention to you."(Henry J. M. Nouwen. A Cry for Mercy.)

In my last year of seminary, I had a "great dream," which I recorded in my journal:

"I was in a strange city during a large parade. People were standing along the avenues ten deep and watching the parade floats go by. Suddenly, two young men dressed in black rode their bicycles up to a lamp post where I was standing and they began to preach a blasphemous message against Jesus Christ and the church. I challenged them and called them liars. And then I picked up their bicycles and threw them at the young men. They were the devil's disciples, and they began to pursue me with a crowd of people. I jumped over a chain link fence, and in the dream, it was a sunny summer afternoon in Michigan where I once lived.

"I hid in a tool shed in my back yard that had two windows in the garage style doors. The police shined a powerful flashlight into the dark shed, but they could not see me. They did this twice, but they could not see me! Then the dream sequence showed me two angels standing in front of me with their wings outstretched making me invisible to the evil ones.

"Next to the angels were two women from the San Mateo Church as witnesses. They were sitting at a card table smiling at me. Then the voice of God spoke and said, 'I am sending the angels ahead of you to protect you on your journey.' My youngest sister Julie was in the dream also, and the voice said, 'She is a chosen vessel of mine, and I have a special place for her."

A year later, in 1981, the dream was fulfilled when Jane and I became urban missionaries in New Orleans. We had a discipleship house for ten men with life controlling problems. We arrived a week before Mardi Gras and watched the parade on Magazine Street near the Irish Channel. We lived in the Irish Channel. the most dangerous slum in New Orleans. Rev. Bill Brown was the director of the para-church ministry to the poor and marginalized. Bill was a Presbyterian minister hired by Dr. Pitman when he was the senior pastor at Canal Street Presbyterian Church. Bill began his own ministry called Trinity Christian Fellowship.

My prophetic dream of angels protecting us and going before us to the strange city was unfolding before our eyes. We arrived in New Orleans pulling a small U-Haul trailer behind our bright yellow, four-speed Volkswagen Rabbit. It was late January, and Mardi Gras was beginning. The Bacchanalian, ten-day revelry originated as a prelude to and preparation for the Roman Catholic season of Lent, forty days of fasting and contrition. It has become a drunken week of parades, promiscuity, and debauchery. Jewish people were not allowed to have a float or participate in Mardi Gras, so they went on vacation and left the city during those ten days.

Jane and I were shocked by the depravity of New Orleans. I had never lived in such an old American city nor one that lived by the Napoleonic code of law instead of English law. It was like living in a foreign country. We were almost the only white people living in the Irish Channel. There were two other couples working with Trinity Christian Fellowship. One couple, Bob and Alma Little, lived a block from our house on Annunciation Street. Bob was a medical doctor with Tulane University. He operated a free medical clinic in the St. Thomas housing project across the street from our house. Jane and I became good friends with the Littles and their two children. Our area was so bad that the police would not come there at night.

Our house on Annunciation st. was called a "shotgun house" because one could fire a gun through the front door, and the bullet would travel out the back door through the kitchen. It was a Greek Revival Style house with no foundation due to the high-water level in

New Orleans. Our little apartment was in the upstairs in the back of the house, which was originally the slave quarters. The house had been built in the 1850s. The servants had been slaves.

Ten men lived in this discipleship house. They were young and old, homeless, and had addictions to drugs and alcohol. Some had criminal records, and others were young men far away from home "sowing their wild oats" in sin city. It had the unfortunate name of the "House of the Risen Son." Of course, we received many calls from drunks in the middle of the night inquiring about prostitution services at the infamous "House of the Rising Sun," from the notorious ballad.

Jane and I prepared the meals. We had a fresh vegetable cooperative at our house one day a week at which our neighbors could buy fresh produce. I led the weekly devotions and bible study and counseled with the men. We had strict rules about alcohol use, and all the men had to work during the day. They were also required to attend church on Sunday and a Friday night prayer and praise celebration at a Catholic Charismatic parish in the French Quarter. The pastor of this church was Father La France. The 250-year-old building was a Carmelite monastery and had domed archways painted with angels. The church was bathed in prayer by the Carmelite sisters. I could feel the Presence of the Holy Spirit in it as soon as I entered. It reminded me of St. Teresa of Avila, the reformer of the Carmelite monasteries in Spain in the 16th century. It brought to mind her writings about "union with God" and her raptures and mystical transports in the Spirit.

This Irish Channel ministry was both difficult and dangerous. Our apartment was robbed while the director was downstairs doing an interview with a magazine reporter. Jane and I lost some class rings and jewelry. A man was murdered by a drunken couple two houses down the street from us. One night shortly after we arrived in New Orleans, I looked out from our second floor apartment and saw a black man in his long johns carrying a hunting rifle running after another man. Jane said, "Should we call the police?" "No," I said. "They would not come here at night because it is too dangerous for them."

We did not have many success stories, but there was one that was noteworthy. A young man had been told about our house and that he would be able to stay for free. Dolph Bell did not look like the other men in the house. He was handsome with curly brown hair and a winning smile. He was 21 years old, just barely out of high school. He had come from Virginia to the party city of New Orleans for a good time. All his money had been spent on women and wild living in the French Quarter. In short, he was a modern day "prodigal son" straight out of the Gospel of Luke 15: 11-32.

Jesus told this parable about a wealthy young man who demanded that his father give him his inheritance. The son "squandered his property in reckless living." Dolph was in rebellion, which the prophet Samuel said is like the sin of witchcraft. He was certainly in the right place for that. New Orleans has a long history of witches and black magic Voodoo.

Many who came to the "House of the Risen Son" were demonized. We prayed for these men on a regular basis. Some men refused to stay in our house because the demons knew we would cast them out by the power of Jesus and the Holy Spirit. Dolph was a prodigal son, but after several months with us, his heart began to soften. He was particularly fond of Jane, as a son would be of a mother. I felt it was time to ask Dolph to write a letter to his parents and let them know he was at our discipleship house in New Orleans. Though not on good terms with his parents, Dolph agreed to write the letter.

A week later, I received a call from Virginia. Dolph's parents were glad he was safe but did not believe he was really changing nor that he had become a Christian. He had put them through great pain and turmoil in his adolescence. Shortly after this phone call, the Bells came to see Dolph. They invited Jane and me to dinner in the French Quarter. Dr. Bell and his wife were very formal and detached, so the dinner was a bit awkward. They had been hurt by Dolph's rejection of them and their lifestyle as conservative Christians. Dr. Bell was a prominent surgeon. Dolph came from a wealthy southern family.

Dolph's parents were friendly, but on their guard. Perhaps they thought we might be a cult or some fringe Christian group. I believe they were shocked by the inner city of New Orleans and especially where we lived in the Irish Channel. Our house was located between two bars, which some of the older men would visit on their way home from work. After all, who would live with the refuse of humanity between Bubber's Bar and another dive doing Christian outreach? I understood their skepticism.

Nevertheless, Dolph had become a born again believer in Jesus Christ before his parents' visit. Jane and I had prayed a simple prayer with him: "Lord Jesus, I surrender my life to you. I know that I am a sinner and that you died on a Roman cross for my sins and the sins of the whole world. I accept you, Jesus, as Lord of my life, and I believe you rose from the dead and that you reign in Heaven with the Father God. Fill me with the Holy Spirit. I renounce all unclean spirits and the devil, in the mighty name of Jesus Christ.

I was able to tell Dolph's parents that their prayers had been answered because of God's grace and mercy for the lost. I reminded them of Jesus's parable of the "prodigal son." I reminded them that when the son came to his senses and returned home, his father had a party for him, killed the fatted calf, and put the ring on his finger indicating that he was still in the family and not a servant. The parable ends with these words: "It was fitting to celebrate and be glad, for thus your brother was dead, and is alive; he was lost and is found."[1]

Dolph stayed with us a few more months, and then he returned to his home in Virginia. He enrolled in Liberty University, a Christian college in Lynchburg, Virginia. He graduated and married a coed he met there. They have several children and are living as a Christian family today.

Not all of our stories end this well. Most of the men were not interested in healing their souls with the blood of Jesus. They remained "dead in their sins and trespasses." Contrary to popular myth, most people become Christians before they reach 20 years of age. There are very few deathbed conversions. Sin has a way of hardening one's soul.

When the Holy Spirit gave me the prophetic dream about a distant city that had many demons and territorial spirits, I did not understand that I would be involved in heavy spiritual warfare. The San Mateo

---

[1] Luke 15:32 ESV.

Church had deliverance teams to deal with demon expulsions, and I had been involved in this ministry as well. There I received valuable training that the theological seminary failed to provide because they did not even believe in the existence of demons or angels. There had been only one professor with whom I could speak about such matters. Herman Waetjen, the Robert S. Dollar chair of the Greek department, had spent time in Africa and had seen demons at work.

During my training at SFTS, I did do one service in Stewart Chapel in which I preached on the reality of the devil and demons and the spiritual warfare in my pastoral work at the Presbyterian church in San Mateo from 1979-1980. One student came up to us after the service to express her gratitude. Dr. Gerry Phelps had been in prison for eight years in Houston, Texas, for robbing a liquor store to fund an underground newspaper. She had been a professor at the University of Houston where she taught a course on Marxism. She was also an outspoken critic of the mayor of Houston.

While in prison, Gerry spent one year in solitary confinement, during which time she had many experiences with demons speaking to her and imitating dead relatives as she searched for God. After her release, she was called to minister to the poor and homeless. She founded a 108-bed facility for the homeless in the Central Valley of California. When she moved to San Jose, she began another mission to homeless people in Santa Clara County. Despite all the wealth in Silicon Valley, the city fathers fought Gerry in her efforts to help the homeless. Standing before me was a brilliant Marxist professor, who had spent eight years in prison, who was working with the "poorest of the poor" because Jesus had bid her to come with Him and give shelter to "the least of my brethren." She was expressing appreciation for my sermon. Later, she preached for me at Santa Rita Jail in Dublin, California, where I was chaplain from 1988 to 2000.

God helped us a great deal in New Orleans. He sent us Walter Hackney, a former high school wrestling champion who was a graduate of Gordon Conwell Seminary. While very smart, Walter was also very strong, standing six feet tall and weighing 240 pounds. He was a good man to have at the house and became a close friend.

The Spirit also brought to our aid a young family, the Dodges. Peter Dodge was heir to French Market Coffee. He worked for the family-owned company in New Orleans. Peter and his wife Ginger were very kind to us and took us on a long weekend to his father's hunting lodge on the West Pearl River in the bayou. We ate blue crab, swam, and went looking for alligators in a flat-bottomed boat. Peter had been delivered from an addiction to marijuana, which he had grown in the middle of his courtyard in New Orleans. One day after work, God spoke to Peter audibly: "Marijuana is an occult god. You are not to worship it." Peter obeyed the voice of God and threw away bales of pot that he had stored in the attic of his house. Though it was worth a great deal of money, Peter was obedient to the voice and destroyed the idol.

After ten months of hard work and sacrifice at Trinity Christian Fellowship, we were discharged by the director, Bill Brown. He did not give us a reason. After I had been there six months, he had hired a young man from Jackson Seminary in Mississippi. He placed this man of limited experience over me, and though I tried, I could not work with him. This may have been Bill Brown's intention all along. So, we left New Orleans in the middle of the night towing a small U-Haul and headed back to California. Our urban missionary work was done, and we were eager to return home.

On the way, we stopped in Tulsa, Oklahoma, to visit Gordon and Susan Wright of Jesus Inn Ministries. They had helped us in New Orleans with a team of evangelists who came during Mardi Gras. Gordon had several discipleship houses on Xanthus Street in Tulsa. They also did outreach to eastern Europe and countries that were closed to the gospel during the Soviet reign of terror. Gordon was a prophet and taught in the bible schools of the underground churches. We still receive Christmas cards from Gordon and Susan.

For a long time, I felt bad about the sudden end of our inner city ministry. Eventually, I realized that God had sent us there and protected us while we were there. The safest place in life to be is in the center of God's will. On several occasions, men in cars nearly abducted Jane while riding her bike. On one occasion, she ran into the Sailors' Union Building near our house to escape them. My encounter was with the two men in black, Satan's workers, whom I had seen in my dream. I came upon them in the French Quarter after attending the Charismatic Catholic service on a Friday night. I had just walked out of the large wooden doors through the wrought iron gate and into the street when two men, dressed all in black, walked past me. They turned around and in unison said, "Satan's!" I responded by shouting, "You have been defeated by Jesus!" They just kept walking into the dark night of the French Quarter.

VIII
Zahra and the Prophet

"I prophecy to you, we are the generation that God will see two streams come together: the stream of the fire of God that comes back into the Church that will purge His people like a refiner's fire; and the stream of supernatural signs and wonders." (Morris Cerullo, The Prophet's Mantle)

Zahra Khalili-Sabet and her son Hooman came into our lives like a Sirocco windstorm. They came to America from Iran via London and Detroit on the pretext of a vacation, a vacation that would turn out to be a life-changing opportunity for herself and her four year old son. She was a true sojourner to America. As Providence would have it, they became our neighbors in Belmont, California, in the summer of 1980.

The given reasons for this "vacation" were visits with a high school friend from Tehran currently living in San Mateo and a nephew living in Jackson, Michigan. Her real reason was to escape a bad marriage. Zahra had met her husband when they were students in Germany. When they married and returned to Tehran, he became very controlling. At times, he would not even speak to her for as long as two months. In Iran, even before the Shah fled the country, a woman needed the permission of her husband to travel alone. His response to her request was, "You will come crawling back to me."

Zahra was a banker at the Tehran International Airport and supervised many employees. She was also a very good businesswoman and had managed to save money for her trip to California in the event her husband ever gave her permission. Being a devout Shiite Muslim, Zahra followed the Quran and had sworn allegiance to Allah and believed that Mohammad was the prophet of God. This was one of the five pillars of faith that every Muslim ascribed to. She did not doubt her faith, but she did doubt her marriage. She strained against her lack of freedom as a woman. She did not want Hooman growing up in Iran with role models like the Revolutionary Guard, which Hooman would one day be pressured to join.

Finally, the day came when she was granted permission to visit her nephew and her friend. In September of 1978, Zahra and Hooman arrived with a tourist visa in hand. Their money was in short supply. Zahra was desperate, but she believed in America as the land of freedom.

I recorded Zahra's story as she told it to me on June 2, 1980. A member of the First Presbyterian Church of San Mateo, who had met Zahra at a Heidi's Pies restaurant, told her about the church and invited her to attend. She thought, "I am a Muslim, and I am not interested in being a Christian, but I could practice my English there, and Hooman could play with the children." At the church, she was introduced to the pastor, Rev. Bob Pitman, in May of 1980. Bob asked if he could pray for her, and she agreed. Rev. Pitman took them into the library, and he prayed that Jesus would bless her and her son and give them guidance. Rev. Pitman did not know that Zahra had thought about committing suicide three times because her life as an immigrant had been so difficult.

That night, Zahra had a prophetic dream. When she later told me of the dream, I was amazed. The Prophet who approached her in the dream was Jesus. To me, this was a clear sign that God was with her and was blessing her. Zahra's account of the dream was as follows:

"I was in a great castle courtyard standing with other Muslim women along a wall with iron bars. The armed soldiers were commanding us to go into a room and change into long, black robes and veils to cover our faces, which was a Sharia law requirement. I did not want to go and change clothes. Suddenly, a man with beautiful eyes and a short beard came up to me from the other side of the tall wall with iron bars and said, "What do you want?" "I want to be free and escape Iran," she replied. The man smiled, looked into her eyes, and said, "Okay." Zahra thought to herself, 'Why can't I have a religion like this?' After the prophet spoke to me in such a loving and nonjudgmental way, I was floating in the air as light as a feather."

When Zahra awoke from the dream, her entire bedroom was filled with the aroma of roses and beautiful, fragrant flowers, like lilies of the valley and the Rose of Sharon. Zahra felt that she had been touched by God in the dream. She called Bob Pitman and asked him to come to her apartment and to bring his wife. A Muslim woman cannot be alone with a man who is not her husband. Bob and Marilyn came and again prayed for Zahra and Hooman. Bob also told her that a member of the church worked for a savings and loan bank in Belmont and may be able to get her a job.

Zahra's search for a job was initially difficult because she spoke with a heavy accent. It became much more difficult when the Ayatollah Khomeini deposed the Shah. After this event, Sharia law governed Iran, and Zahra could never return to her homeland. She did not have a green card, and her future in America was uncertain. Matters became even worse when Khomeini and his soldiers took captive 52 Americans at the American Embassy in Tehran on November 4, 1979. President Carter had been unable to negotiate with the Ayatollah, who hated Christians and especially hated Jimmy Carter. Feelings in America were very strong against Iranians and Shiite Muslims, and Zahra was one of "them."

The church member at the savings and loan that Bob Pitman had said might be able to get her a job was my wife, Jane. Jane told the bank manager that she would be glad to train the new employee. That was the beginning of a long friendship between Zahra and Hooman and the Lynches. Zahra became a regular attendee at the First Presbyterian Church. John Linquist, who had been a missionary in Africa, and his wife Marguerite gave Zahra a bible that had been translated into Persian. As Zahra read God's Word, she began to see the darkness, the veil, fall away from her eyes.

Jane and I invited Zahra and Hooman to our apartment for barbequed hamburgers. I asked Zahra if she was ready to invite Jesus into her life as her Lord and Savior. She said, "Yes." Jane and I prayed with her, and she confessed that Jesus was Lord and beside Him there was no other God. It was the exact opposite of Islam's claim that "God is Allah and Mohammad is his prophet." Zahra had been reading the little brown New Testament that I had given to her. The Holy Spirit opened her eyes to the truth that Jesus is Lord and is coming back a second time to take us into His Father's house in heaven[1]. Instead of feeling suicidal, Zahra felt "light as a feather."

Hooman became my Godson. He was raised in the church and became a fine Christian man. Zahra is a retired accountant and still lives in San Mateo. This was all made possible by a dream whereby Jesus came and smiled and looked into Zahra's eyes and said, "You can be free." In the Gospel of John, the apostle writes, "So if the Son sets you free, you will be free indeed."[2]

Zahra was one of the first Shiite Muslims to convert to Christianity in America. In his great love and mercy, God called this Shiite Muslim to himself through the prayers of a pastor and visions in the night. In her sojourn to America, Zahra became familiar with the "wormwood and the gall" of Jeremiah the prophet. But the weeping prophet also received the promise of salvation that Zahra would also come to know: "It is good for a man that he wait quietly for the salvation of the Lord. It is good for a man that he bear the yoke in his youth."[3]

---

[1] John 14:1-3.

[2] John 8:36 ESV.

[3] Lam. 3 26-27 ESV.

IX
Linda's Sunday Angels and Devils

*"Were it not for the angel hosts empowered by God to resist the demons
of Satan, who could ever hope to press through the battlements of the
fiendish demons of darkness to the Lord of eternal liberty and salvation?"*
(Billy Graham, Angels, God's Secret Agents)

Linda was my younger sister. When I was a senior in high school, she was a freshman. I didn't see Linda in High School as she attended a new school across the parking lot. Because of my father's animosity toward my sister, she retreated inwardly and had a great deal of anger which she expressed.

Our father, Jeff, a southern man full of both pride and prejudice, was also a bipolar manic-depressive with a mean streak. His anger was directed toward Linda and me. We could never do anything right, which greatly affected our self-esteem and confidence. My eighth grade basketball coach once stopped a practice game when I was about to jump for the tip-off. He asked me, in front of the team, "Why don't you ever smile?" I muttered that "I don't know why I don't smile." I was embarrassed and shy. I knew that my home life was awful, but how could I explain that to a coach who had no idea what a manic-depressive could be like?

My father, Jefferson Davis Lynch, was named after the president of the Confederacy by his father. He was not mentally ill when my mother married him in 1946. They met in Denver, Colorado, when he was attending Denver University. He was a very bright person. In the army, his IQ tested at 130 points. His manic-depression was "latent," which means it emerged gradually around the age of 30. Mental illness was not discussed in families and was not readily diagnosed by medical doctors at that time. Lithium carbonate, a salt-based drug and later an effective treatment, was not available yet either. So, my mother became my father's therapist, but also his protector and enabler.

Linda was only 15 years old when I left home for college. I got away from a home that was not a happy place, but she was stuck there with our crazy father. He directed all of his negative criticisms at Linda. She was a victim of mental abuse primarily, which can be more harmful than physical abuse, but that also occurred. Her only defense, aside from our mother who tried to moderate the situation and often failed, was to run away from home. Linda took this evasive action several times before she was 18 years old.

One warm summer day in June of 1971, my father became irate at Linda, pulled out a 12 gauge shotgun, and chased her around the small house screaming at her, "I am going to shoot you!" Linda believed him and ran for her life. She locked her bedroom door, opened the window, and climbed out of the house. She walked to Lapeer Road, a block away, and began to hitchhike north. A friendly man picked her up. He was going to Bay City, Michigan, which was 45 miles northeast of Flint. Linda had no money and, of course, cell phones had not yet been invented. Linda knew our father was crazy and angry, had a shotgun, and was seriously ill. She could not trust her fate to him. She told the man, "Let's go. I want to leave this place."

Jeff's rampage occurred on a Saturday, so my sister planned to not return while he was at home. She was dropped off at a park on the waterfront of Lake Huron. She was afraid, but at least she was alive. A friend had given her a paperback book, *The Electric Kool-Aid Acid Test* by Tom Wolfe. My sister did not do LSD or any hard drugs, but she did smoke pot. My father's manic states made Wolfe's book seem almost comical to her.

She found a bathroom at the park that had running water and a security lamp pole, which she camped under as it grew dark. She stayed there all night reading her book and wondering what she could do next. Early the next morning, a couple of boys camping out on an island in the river came over to talk to this 16 year-old girl. They said, "If we had known you were here by yourself; we would have asked you to join us at our camp." Linda thought, "There is no way I am going to camp out with two teenage boys in the middle of a river!"

As the sun began to rise above Lake Huron early on Sunday morning, a well-dressed man appeared suddenly before Linda, startling her. The man said to her, "You need to call home! You need to call home!" In her most defiant tone, she replied, "I don't have a dime." The man handed her a dime for the pay phone and said, "Go home. It will be okay." She obeyed the man and called home. Her mother answered the phone, and Linda asked if Jeff was still going to shoot her. Her mother replied, "No, it will be okay." An hour later, her parents arrived to pick her up from the park by the river. They took her to a drive-in restaurant because she had not eaten in 24 hours.

Two years later, my sister joined the army, lost weight, and became a soldier. The Vietnam War was winding down, and females were not sent to Vietnam in a combat capacity. So, Linda spent two years going to classes and getting a salary to learn new things. When the war ended in 1975, Linda was discharged. She liked North Carolina where she was stationed, so she applied to a college, Atlantic Christian, and was enrolled in a teaching program. Her mother was a teacher, and Linda followed in her footsteps. The GI Bill covered all four years of her college education. During her college days, she lived in a trailer in Wilson, North Carolina. She had been raised in the Baptist church, so she believed in God, but she did not know God in a personal way. Not yet.

On November 4, 1979, I called my mother to talk with her and see how the family was doing. I later entered in my journal what she reported to me regarding Linda and her two visions: I later entered in my journal what she reported to me regarding Linda and her two visions:

"This afternoon, I called mom in Flint, MI, and we had an interesting chat! She told me that my sister, Linda, who lives in Wilson, NC, had two visions. In the first vision, a beautiful woman with curly dark hair and a black dress came to her and asked my sister for 'her soul.' My sister was terrified and said, 'The blood of Jesus covers my soul.' A second beautiful blonde woman came to my sister and again asked for her soul, and once again my sister said, 'The blood of Jesus covers my soul.' The two women laughed at Linda and jabbed at her with a two-edged sword that they carried. The women threatened to kill Linda with the sword. The two women would not go away until my sister began praying in tongues mentally to herself and God. To her amazement the two demons left her. But they left behind them a pair of black shoes!"

A neighbor friend of Linda's invited her to see a film about the life of the Rev. David Wilkerson, "The Cross and the Switchblade." Since she was still very perplexed and afraid of the visions she had recently seen, she agreed to see the film. After the film, the neighbor invited Linda to her house for coffee. She also invited her son, who was a Pentecostal minister like David Wilkerson. Linda told the minister of her visions, and he suggested she read the Book of Acts, which has dreams and visions in it. Acts 5:12-16 relates the early church's experiences with miracles and healings. Several other people who were present began to pray aloud in tongues (unknown languages given as a gift by the Holy Spirit in Acts 2).

My sister joined them. She had never spoken in tongues out loud before. The minister interpreted the tongue saying, "God is pleased with some areas of your life and displeased with other areas. It is time to 'get your act together.' The two shoes represent your half-hearted attempt at following Jesus and that you must be totally committed to him and not lukewarm."[1]

My mother and father never apologized to my sister for the cruel and violent shotgun episode. They blamed her for being a rebellious teenager. Shortly after that event, the recession of 1974 caused General Motors to force Jeff into retirement. He was still not medicated. His crazy behavior eventually landed him in a locked psychiatric facility 100 miles from home in Ypsilanti, Michigan. It was a week before Christmas. Jeff had disappeared, and Thelma was in a panic. As the heavy medication wore off, Jeff finally remembered his phone number and called home. Thelma got a lawyer and a court order to have him transferred to Hurley Hospital in Flint, which had a psychiatric ward. As Providence would have it, my mother's best friend's husband was a nurse in the psychiatric unit and knew my father. Jeff was stabilized

[1] M.S. Lynch, *Journal*, Monday, Nov. 5, 1979

and diagnosed at last as bi-polar manic-depressive. The psychiatrist prescribed lithium carbonate; the salt-based drug that helps balance the brain chemicals. Jeff was much improved after treatment and no longer had wild mood swings.

Linda has been a teacher of the severely handicapped in Wilson for the last 31 years. In her spare time, she has a puppet ministry at the Four Square Pentecostal Church in Wilson. She travels the state doing evangelism for children and adults through puppetry. Her husband Tom worked as a surveyor. And now is retired. Her son Eric works in computers and animation. Her son Nick is an archeologist. Linda has been blessed greatly by Jesus, and Satan had to relinquish his claim on her soul because it is "covered by the blood of Jesus."

Linda and Tom live in the country in a ranch style home surrounded by several acres of pine trees and flowers.

X
Easter 1988 and a New Ministry

"I see an oval-shaped door with bars and rocks piled all around it calling out: 'We want God! We want God!'" (Prophetic vision of Van Wilson)

I received the good news on April 4, 1988, the Friday before Easter. My unfulfilled pastoral pursuits were about to achieve fruition. The voice on the telephone said, "I am calling you to offer you the position of chaplain at the North County Jail in Oakland, California. Do you accept the job?" I said, "Yes." "When can you start work?" Sondra asked. I answered without hesitation, "On Monday morning." Eight years had passed since my graduation from seminary, and most Christian folks had given up on Jane and me. Apparently, God had not.

This jail was a fairly new facility and just a five minute walk from Jack London Square on the Oakland waterfront. I was the first full-time M-designated manager that Alameda County had hired in many years. This meant I had county benefits and a cafeteria fund for other insurances. The starting salary was $35,000, which at that time was more than a starting teacher's salary. I knew I was seeing the fulfillment of Van Wilson's prophecy of the jailhouse door and the pile of rocks crying out "We want God!"

When I called Jane at Magee Plastics in Menlo Park where she worked, she cried tears of joy. Our first daughter, Monika, was only three years old at the time, and I worked a swing shift at a home for the developmentally disabled adults in Belmont so that I could care for her while Jane worked days.

Over the previous years, I had worked as a volunteer chaplain at San Quentin Prison with Chaplain Bert Russell and Harry Howard, both of whom were legends in prison ministry. I had also been a minister-intern at San Mateo Presbyterian Church and a volunteer at the Redwood City Jail. At last, I was a full chaplain for two facilities in Alameda County. Because the Lutheran chaplain, Wally, had died of cancer three months after I started working for the Sheriff's Department,

I inherited the old jail in Dublin called Santa Rita. Between these two jails, there were more than 3,200 inmates. Though the task seemed overwhelming, I was encouraged by two strong advantages.

First, because of Van Wilson's prophecy, I knew Jesus intended me to be here. The second was Glen Morrison, who trained many of the religious volunteers at Follow Up Ministries, Inc. (FUMI) The Rev. Johnny Jones was working for FUMI at the time, and he acquainted me with what was happening in the jails in a spiritual sense. Glen Morrison came into North County Jail every Sunday, so I was able to get his guidance as well. Another co-worker at North County Jail and Santa Rita Jail was Frank Beville, a Roman Catholic Deacon from Catholic Charities in Oakland. Frank was a Catholic Charismatic from St. Leander Catholic Church in San Leandro. He was a man of God and very gifted as a chaplain. We became good friends.

From 1988 to 1994, there was a continuous revival happening in the jails. The Holy Spirit was blowing out the old cobwebs that Satan had spun and was replacing them with a fresh anointing of Jesus and the power of the resurrection from the dead. So many inmates were saved from their lives of sin and chaos that we ran out of bibles and Christian materials. At Santa Rita, I discovered a room stacked with bibles and other materials just gathering dust. My first action as head chaplain was to have jail trustees take boxes of bibles to the lockup units and give them away. Since I had no budget for religious materials, I petitioned the Sheriff for money from the Inmate Welfare Fund. This fund contained several million dollars, all generated from jail telephones and snack bars. I pointed out how unfair it was to deny a prisoner freedom of religion by denying them bibles and Qurans. Our cause was aided by passage of the Religious Freedom Restoration Act of 1993 (RFRA), introduced as a bill into the House of Representatives by Chuck Schumer and into the Senate by Ted Kennedy, signed into law by President Bill Clinton in 1993. This legislation provided inmates with attorneys if they were denied religious liberties.

I split time between NCJ and Santa Rita during the week. During the first couple weeks of my employment, the Holy Spirit sent me a sign of the deep spiritual hunger at Santa Rita Jail. Late one afternoon,

I was working in my office, which was located next to the "weight pile," when a deputy sheriff called me and asked me to see an inmate who was in crisis. Despite being extremely tired at the end of a long, hot summer day, I agreed to see Greg Bell. Greg walked down the dusty road past the chain link fences and compounds filled with prisoners to the white, clapboard chapel topped with the iron cross bearing the crucified Jesus. He knocked on my door. He sat down and immediately began to weep. I asked him what was wrong. He said the judge had said he was going to send him to state prison if Greg ever appeared before him again. Greg had been involved in the entertainment business in Los Angeles and had become addicted to cocaine. His previous convictions had been for possession of cocaine as well. He was an addict!

My counsel to Greg was straightforward and merciful: "Greg, I don't know all that you have done in your life as far as crime and evil, but I know that Jesus will forgive you your sins and heal your life if you surrender right now to the Lordship of Jesus Christ. God still loves you and will make your path straight." Greg continued to cry. I could see he was a broken and contrite person. After we prayed together, he asked me what he was to do about the judge. I told him that a counselor in the East Bay recovery facility had promised to save a bed for me if I ever met an inmate that was ready to change his life. After Greg left my office, I called the Christian counselor, who agreed to accept him into the recovery center. I wrote Greg a letter giving him the information.

The next day, Greg appeared before the judge and gave him my letter with the organization's address. The judge relented and gave Greg a year in the facility. I did not hear from Greg for eight months. When he did call, he said, "I did the entire year in the rehab facility and went to church every Sunday, and I never used cocaine again!" He also told me that he was working for a Christian radio station selling advertisements. He was also arranging meetings for the evangelist Mario Murrillo. I was very excited to be a part of his life, witnessing how the Holy Spirit was transforming a human being. Greg's experience is a testimony of the power of God, which the apostle Paul described in his letter to the Romans:

"There is therefore no condemnation for those who are in Christ Jesus. For the law of the Spirit of life has set you free in Christ Jesus from the law of sin and death ... For all who are led by the Spirit of God are sons of God."[1]

Alice, another inmate that made a deep impression on me, was from the new Santa Rita Jail that I helped to open in 1989. This new jail was a modern facility with stainless steel robotic boxes that traveled along tracks that picked up the food from the kitchen and delivered the hot trays to the units all over the jail. It could house 3,000 inmates and had its own water supply and twin diesel generators for emergency back-up power. Nestled in the hills of Dublin, Santa Rita Jail was named after a Catholic patron saint for the poor and oppressed. The name did not fit. The new jail still harbored an animosity toward the inmates. Time served was still "hard time."

Alice's story is one of Satanic bondage that was generational in her family. She was a third-generation witch. She was of German ancestry, and both her mother and grandmother were witches. For her family, witchcraft was serious business. The other female inmates were justifiably afraid of Alice. She possessed spiritual gifts from Satan. She could predict future events, such as earthquakes, and knew the evil spirits who lived in the other women in the jail. She knew them by name.

When I first met Alice, she had a roommate who was a lesbian and had the HIV virus. Alice had put a request in to the chaplain's office to talk to me about her two children. When I entered the recreation area where the visit was to take place, I had difficulty breathing. The unclean spirits made the room very cold. I knew I was dealing with some very powerful evil spirits living in Alice. However, Alice had some troubling concerns about the Satanist group she belonged to in San Francisco. She feared they might get her children and use them in ritualistic ceremonies. Alice still had the mother's instinct to save her children. She told me she had hidden her children in another state for their protection from the Satanists. She had herself been badly abused by the occult witchcraft group, despite being very intelligent.

[1] Rom 8:1-2; 14 ESV

Nevertheless, Jesus and the angels of heaven were of no interest to Alice. Her only interest was the fallen angels that she had been subject to her entire life. She was a fund raiser, embezzler, and expert in disguises for the Satanist church, the real cult that practiced blood sacrifices and summoned evil spirits. It seemed all I could do for her was pray. I visited with Alice for eight months with not much success in helping her to see the Light of Jesus Christ. I knew that spiritual warfare was going on, and that these evil spirits could be defeated only through prayer.[2] Fortunately, I knew of a prayer warrior! Barbara was a Christian volunteer from Follow Up Ministries. I asked her to visit with Alice, though I doubted that such a child of darkness and slave to Satan would ever be free. I was wrong.

One day Barbara burst into my office and said, "Chaplain, you won't believe what has happened! Alice became a Christian." I said, "You are correct. I don't believe it." I went to see for myself. Before I could say anything, Alice told me what had happened to her. The witch had become a Believer in Jesus Christ as Lord, resurrected from the dead and coming King. The following testimony was written by Alice and given to me as a true record of her conversion to Jesus Christ:

———— •《◉》• ————

A Testimony by Alice as told to Chaplain Lynch

"My name is Alice, and I am incarcerated in Santa Rita Jail in Dublin, California. I am being held in the maximum security section of the jail. I referred to my cell in a poem that I recently wrote as "the belly of hell where I am eaten alive by each turn of the brass key." I kept my cell dark, blotting out the light by erecting a cardboard and paper barrier over my slender steel and plexiglass window. I was a child of the night!

---

[2] M.S. Lynch, *Prayer Journal*, May 16, 1989. "Set the captives free! Bind Satan our adversary. Deliver Alice from the clutches of the occult group. Bring freedom upon her through Jesus Christ who came to destroy the works of the devil. Heal us, Oh Lord, from the ravages of sin and Satan."

"On March 2, 1990, I began to notice the darkness of my life. This was to be the greatest day of my life! For on this day, I became a child of God and was delivered from the bondage of Satan. My life had been a long and lonely journey. I was so depressed that the psychiatrist put me on medication. In February, I wrote a poem where I described myself in third person: 'Her mind is now full of garbage sloshing around in madness-- orgasms of thought by the big brass key--turned by mindless vengeance and bondage. For the lock and key, murder has control: pure and raw, lustful violence. That is all that can live in the belly of hell as the big brass key turns to lock me in forever.'

"I had my only window covered with paper, so no light entered my 7'x10' cell. I was used to the darkness! But suddenly a deputy barked an order at me, "Remove the blockage from your window!" The female officer had seen this window covered before, but never had said anything to me. When she spoke to me, Jesus also spoke those words to me in a spiritual sense. As I tore down the paper barrier, the light of day streamed into my cell. I got down on my knees and asked Jesus to enter my life and be my personal Savior! His cleansing blood washed me and took away my sins and guilt. I knew immediately that I was "born again." The darkness had no more power over me for now I was a child of light. The Holy Spirit of God has come to me, and I have everlasting life! Praise the Lord!

"My old god, Satan, loosed his hellish fury upon me, for I was his servant all of my life. The devil still comes to me in dreams at night. He tempts me through inmates and police alike. The thoughts he puts in my mind are full of lies and blasphemies! But try as he may, Satan the Destroyer has lost! I am free, and I am happy in Jesus Christ the Lord. God has shown me my old life, and he has removed the scales from my eyes. I am attracted to the bible and to prayer, and I cling to these graces.

"The Holy Spirit began to convict me of sin. Another female inmate was making overtures toward me to have sex with her. We were in the clinic, and I told her that I am a 'born again' Christian, and I am not into lesbianism anymore! The cursing of other inmates bothers me more now that I am all 'new creature in Christ.' I feel more sensitive, and my conscience is being restored. I have begun to share the Gospel with others, and I am praying in my jail cell every chance I get. I used to think that the chaplain and the religious volunteers were all crazy. But now I know that Jesus said, 'You shall know the truth, and the truth shall set you free.' I love God now, and he loves me! Now I can love myself, too! I smile a lot these days despite my captivity. THANK YOU, JESUS. AMEN."

Shortly after Alice's amazing conversion to Jesus, her satanic-priest brother came to visit her at Santa Rita Jail. The priest had heard that Alice was a Christian, and he did not believe it. Alice told her brother, who had worshiped Satan all his life, that she was "born again in the Holy Spirit." She told him that Jesus has conquered the grave, hell, and death. Alice told me, "My brother left disgusted because he could tell that I had a different spirit than his."

I rejoiced with Alice, my new sister in the Lord. Over the years, I have lost touch with her, but I still pray for her and her two children that the spiritual, generational bondage be broken forever. I think of Peter's advice to the Christians in Rome who were experiencing persecution around 65 AD. He encouraged them with these words:

> "Be sober-minded; be watchful. Your adversary the devil prowls around like a roaring lion, seeking someone to devour. Resist him firm in your faith, knowing that the same kinds of suffering are being experienced by your brotherhood throughout the world. And after you have suffered a little while, the God of all grace, who has called you to His eternal glory in Christ, will himself restore, confirm, strengthen, and establish you. To him be the dominion forever and ever. Amen."[3]

This account by Alice was given to me by the author, Alice, and is completely truthful. I witnessed her transformation in Christ Jesus the Lord. Alice was in jail for eleven months before she accepted Jesus as her Savior. Jesus set her free from her slavery to evil spirits and Satan.

Years earlier, while I was in seminary, Dr. Gerry Phelps told me of the prisoners in the Houston, Texas, prison who were demonized.

---

[3] 1 Peter 5:8-11 ESV.

Gerry was set free from evil spirits by reading God's Word and by the complete surrender of her life to Jesus. The theologian Karl Barth has said, "Wherever the Word is proclaimed and obeyed, there is the Church." The gates of Hell cannot overcome the true Church of Jesus Christ!

XI
Angels and Demons

"The failure to understand the demonic dimension to the Christian's sin problem is perhaps the weak point, the Achilles' heel, in our Evangelical theology of evil and temptation ...." (Ed Murphy, Director of International Ministry Team of Overseas Crusades)

Angels and demons know who we are and can either hinder us or help us depending upon in whom we place our faith. All the angels were created by God. The Godhead did not create angels because he was lonely or bored. YHWH, the I AM that I AM, created angels for his pleasure and joy. He also created the angels to reflect his Glory and his Splendor. According to the bible, mankind was created a little lower than the angels and certainly with much less power and authority. By definition, angels are "minds without bodies," according to Mortimer Adler in his book, *The Angels and Us*. There are six orders of angels in medieval theology: Seraphim, Cherubim, Thrones, Dominations, Virtues, and Powers.[1] Dr. Adler never claimed to be a Christian, but as a philosopher, he studied Thomas Aquinas, who was the theologian of angelology. The angels are listed in order of importance of their service to the most high God.

The last group of angels is Powers and Authorities. "These angels protect us against evil influences, and they order our affairs," according to Adler. Part of this group are the Principalities, who protect cities and nations. For example, the Archangel Michael is Prince and Protector of God's people and gives messages to men and women from God.[2] King David wrote Psalm 34 when he feigned madness before King Abimelech to save his own life. In the Psalm, David states, "This poor man called, and the Lord heard him: he saved him out of all his troubles. The

---

[1] Mortimer Adler, *The Angels and Us* (New York: Macmillan, 1982), 50-51.
[2] *Ibid.*

angel of the Lord encamps around those who fear him, and he delivers them."[3]

Charles Spurgeon, in Volume 1 of his great commentary entitled *The Treasury of David*, quotes Zachary Bogan regarding this passage:

"But this godly man may assure himself of, that whatsoever he shall want their help, in spite of doors, and locks, and bars, he may have it in a moment's warning. For there is no impediment, either for power because they are spirits, or for want of good will, both because it is their duty, and because they bear an affection in him; not only rejoicing at his conversion,[4] but, I dare confidently affirm, always disposed with abundance of cheerfulness to do anything for him."[5]

The demons or fallen angels are discussed in two main sections of the Old Testament, Isaiah 14:12-17 and Ezekiel 28:12-19. Satan's fall from heaven is described metaphorically as a taunt against the King of Babylon:

"How you are fallen from heaven, 0 Day Star, son of Dawn! How you are cut down to the ground, you who laid the nations low! You said in your heart, 'I will ascend to heaven; above the stars of God, I will set my throne on high; I will sit on the mount of assembly in the far reaches of the north; I will ascend above the heights of the clouds; I will make myself like the Most High.'"[6]

In the Ezekiel scripture, the prophet uses metaphor in his condemnation of the Prince of Tyre, whom he personifies as Lucifer, a Covering Cherub, who was the most beautiful of all God's creation. Theologians believe that Lucifer, which means the "shining or bright one," was in charge of all praise and worship in heaven. Lucifer's sin

---

[3] Ps. 34:6-7.

[4] Luke 15:10.

[5] Charles Spurgeon, *The Treasury of David*, vol. 1 (Peabody: Hendrickson, 1988), 129-130.

[6] Is. 14:12-17 ESV.

was one of pride in that he desired to be worshiped like God. Ezekiel states:

> "You were blameless in your ways from the day you were created, till unrighteousness was found in you. In the abundance of your trade, you were filled with violence in your midst, and you sinned; I cast you as a profane thing from the mountain of God, and I destroyed you, O Guardian Cherub, from the midst of the stones of fire. Your heart was proud because of your beauty."[7]

In my vocation and calling as a chaplain and ordained minister of the Gospel of Christ, I have had many encounters with evil spirits and demonic powers. During my minister internship at San Mateo First Presbyterian Church, Jane and I were involved in exorcisms, prayers for healing, and deliverance from demons in church attendees as well as neopagans. It is no wonder that in the rite of baptism, many Christian churches also pray for Christians to be "delivered from evil spirits" as an element of the sacrament. I prayed for this for every prisoner that I baptized at the jails.

The Book of Common Prayer of the Episcopal Church, 1945 edition, states the following regarding the baptism of children: "Dost thou, therefore, in the name of this child, renounce the devil and all his works, the vain pomp and glory of the world, with all covetous desires of the same, and the sinful desires of the flesh, so that thou wilt not follow, nor be led by them?"[8] I have used this admonition in baptizing inmates in the county jail. Some men were serial killers, and others were followers of the devil. Nevertheless, when they "confessed with their mouths and believed in their heart that Jesus has risen from the dead, they were saved."[9] In the baptismal vows, I always have the person renounce Satan and all his works of iniquity. These holy sacraments of baptism and marriage are commanded by Jesus in the scriptures and are to be taken seriously. The Real Presence of Jesus abides in these sacraments.

---

[7] Ezek. 28:15-17a ESV.

[8] *The Book of Common Prayer,* 1945 ed., 276.

[9] Rom. 10:9 ESV.

I believe in guardian angels sent by Jesus to protect the elect of God. My mother named me after Michael the Archangel who fought on behalf of Daniel against the Prince of Persia after he had prayed for 21 days. The angels do spiritual warfare on our behalf. An example of this from my own life occurred in 1985. I had been terminated from a job as a counselor in a halfway house in San Mateo. My firstborn daughter, Monika, had just been born on October 15, 1985. My wife, Jane, was staying home with the new baby, and I had no health insurance. Furthermore, we were working with the San Francisco Vineyard Church hosting a home church at our house in Burlingame. I was working part-time jobs wherever I could find work. Jane was very emotional and under stress during this time. As I lay sleeping, Jane was awake watching a visible, three-dimensional spiritual battle taking place above our bed. My account from a journal relates this amazing encounter with angels and demons:

"Jane's bedroom vision of angels and grotesque looking animal spirits occurred in the space above our bed! The demons were trying to destroy our marriage and us. I was asleep and Jane did not wake me until it was over. I remember sensing something in the room that was really strange. Jane said, 'The demons were without weapons, but the angels were all carrying weapons and armor.' The angels from God had the authority of the 'name that is above all names.' Satan's forces are without the weapons of God. They were defeated by myriads of angels in full battle array! They carried the sword of the Spirit!"[10]

Jane's vision of the great battle of angels and demons in our bedroom gave me extra courage. I realized that as Christians we are clothed with power and the "helmet of salvation and the shield of faith with the sword of the Spirit." Paul's analogy in his letter to the Ephesians 6:10-18 is not merely symbolic; it is a reality in the spirit world. This wild scene above our bed occurred during a time of economic turmoil and uncertainty in our lives. We prevailed in this intense spiritual warfare by means of prayer, reading the Word of God, and angelic intervention. Jesus is quoted in Matthew: "Take heed that you do not despise one of

[10] M.S. Lynch, Journal, September 23, 1999.

these little ones, for I say to you that in heaven their angels see the face of My Father who is in heaven."[11]

"Little ones" does not mean children, as commonly believed, but rather "humble believers." The word in Greek for little is micron and may mean least important, insignificant, or humble. Jesus uses this word three times in the verses from Matt. 18:6, 10, 14, in his discourse on "punishment for offenders." It is quite clear that the Lord Jesus Christ confirmed the Jewish belief in guardian angels.

In my younger, pagan days, just prior to my conversion to Jesus Christ in November of 1971, I was partying with friends and driving in the country. I had been drinking beer and using drugs. The combination of these two intoxicants made me violently ill to the point of near death. "Stop the car!" I shouted to Randy, the driver. I jumped out of the car and stumbled into a freshly tilled farmer's field, because I did not want to die in a smelly old car. I remember looking up into the starry night sky with a full moon and thinking, "I don't want to die here." In a moment, I felt better, and the death spirit left me. I believe the guardian angels saved my life from a drug overdose that night. I believe Satan was trying to take my soul, but he was prevented from doing so because God knew I would believe in Jesus three months later. He sent my guardian angels to help me in my time of vulnerability and sin.

---

[11] Matt.18:10 NKJ.

XII
Vision of the Three Crosses

"En toutoi nika-in this sign, conquer." (Constantine's vision of a flaming cross at the Mulvian Bridge, Oct. 27, 312 AD. Will Durant)

My calling from God as a prophet and teacher was not easy. I was not understood and was largely rejected by the institutional church, both evangelical and liberal. Jane, my dear wife, suffered more than me. She was convinced that I would never have a worthy job and that I was not a good provider. My life was precarious, and I lived on the edge of oblivion. Jane wanted to have children, but without her steady but low paying jobs in banks, we would be homeless. To find solace, I read the Catholic mystics, Meister Eckhart, Teresa of Avila, St. John of the Cross, and the Trappist monk, Thomas Merton. I found the following prayer from Merton, which I glued into my bible:

> "My Lord God, I have no idea where I am going. I do not see the road ahead of me. I cannot know for certain where I will end. Nor do I really know myself, and the fact that I think that I am following your will does not mean that I am actually doing so. But I believe that the desire to please you does in fact please you. And I hope I have that desire in all that I am doing. I hope that I will never do anything apart from that desire! And I know that if I do this you will lead me by the right road though I may know nothing about it. Therefore, will I trust you always though I may seem to be lost and in the shadow of death. I will not fear, for you are ever with me, and you will never leave me to face my perils alone."[1]

On September 1, 1980, I was on call as a pastor from the Presbyterian Church in San Mateo. Everyone else was off for Labor Day. At 3:30 a.m., I received a call from Marilyn Pitman notifying me that there had been a car accident in Foster City and that a sixteen-year-old boy had died. While I went to the hospital for a bereavement

[1] <Thomas Merton, *Thoughts in Solitude, yahoo.comImageResults*>

visit with the mother of this deceased son, Jane had the first of three visions of the Cross of Christ:

"While I was gone, Jane felt like she was going to have to support me as a minister, and she wondered why God didn't give her a career as a doctor, lawyer, or a teacher, etc. All of a sudden God, the Holy Spirit, spoke to her in a short vision. Jane saw Jesus crucified, and she focused on the center of the cross that had LOVE nailed there. Then the Holy Spirit said, 'Did you earn this?'"[2]

The second cross was a visible one in her bedroom as she stepped out of the shower. Jane sensed a presence in the room that startled her. She looked around and saw a two-foot high vaporous cross in perfect dimensions on the large mirror over the sink outside of the bathroom. It was painted by unseen hands. The cross disappeared after a minute, but she understood that Jesus was again reminding her of the cost of bearing the cross of Christ as a disciple for him.

Elie Weisel wrote a best-selling book about his horrific experiences in a Nazi concentration camp during World War II. The book, Night, tells of the horror of six million Jews dying in the gas chambers. Weisel lost his faith in Judaism as a result of his experiences in the Auschwitz labor camp. Jane was reading this book and thinking, "How could a good God allow this satanic evil to destroy his own people?" In my journal of September 3, 1980, I wrote:

"The Lord Jesus showed Jane his cross covering every horror and evil. Humans did not suffer more than the sinless Messiah Jesus. Jesus died for all the sins of the world! Two days later, Jane was wondering how or why she was to support me, and the Lord gave her a vision of LOVE nailed to the center of the cross of Christ. "Did you earn this?" asked the Lord. It was not a put-down but a kind and gentle correction to her confused thinking. It was a rhetorical question that required an answer of "No."[3]

---

[2] M.S. Lynch, *Journal*, Sept. 1, 1980. JANE HAD BEEN ENCOURAGED TO APPLY TO TWO LAW SCHOOLS, Tulane and Hastings in San Francisco because of her high score of 40 on the L..S.A.T. law entrance exam.

[3] Ibid., Sept. 3, 1980.

In my studies with the Jesuit theologian, Father Michael Buckley, I read about God meeting us in the "dark night of the soul" and how we enter into Divine union with God:

> "We may say that there are three reasons for which the journey made by the soul to union with God is called night. The first has to do with the point from which the soul goes forth, for it has gradually to deprive itself of desire for all the worldly things which it possessed, by denying them to itself; the which denial and deprivation are, as it were, night to all the senses of man. The second reason has to do with the mean, or the road along which the soul must travel to this union-that is, faith, which is likewise as dark as night to the understanding. The third has to do with the point to which it travels-namely, God, Who, equally, is dark night to the soul of this life. These three nights must pass through the soul-or, rather, the soul must pass through them-in order that it may come to Divine union with God."[4]

This great LOVE nailed to the cross that Jane saw in visions was to carry her and me through the stormy waters and the tidal wave of mud and slime that Satan threw our way. Sometimes our correct theological ideas and systems must die to realize that God is sacrificial love carried out in Jesus Christ. One of my favorite writers is Teresa of Avila, who wrote in 1577 concerning love: "The important thing is not to think much but to love much; and so, do that which best stirs you to love."[5]

---

[4] St. John of the Cross, *Ascent of Mount Carmel,* trans. and ed. E. Allison Peers (New York: Image Books, 1958), 105-106.

[5] Teresa of Avila, *Interior Castle*, trans. Kieran Kavanaugh and Otilio Rodriguez (New York: Paulist Press, 1979), 70.

Thelma Zoppelli
Denver-1943

Sadie Zoppelli & Thelma Lynch
Baby - Mike Lynch-Dec. 1952

Mike in Palm Springs with
wild friends: Dave & BRAD
1970
Adolph Zoppelli's House

Mike, Linda-Top
Jim, Julie-1969
Lynch

3)

Jane-Tony-Mike-Oct. 2016-
Mule Creek Prison

Bangkok, Thailand
2014
Jane & Mike
Top-center photo

English learners
Class, Santisuk
School

4) Christmas - 1989 - Center Back - Glen ~ Rev.
Morrison
Oakland, Ca. Front - Chaplin Lynch

Prayer And Praise - Left: Jane, Marie & Rick Wilson
2 draft - 3rd Right → San Mateo, 2019 - Linguist's House

2) Marriage Reception, Sept., 1974
Flint, Mich.

Thelma Lynch   Jeff Lynch

1
9
6
6

Teacher At
Barhitte elementary

G.M. Data-
Processing

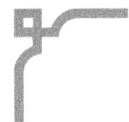

XIII
The Filling of the Holy Spirit

"But no experience ever equaled in bliss the baptism of pure light and power that came to me from God, not through the medium of man's counseling and praying with me, but through the sun and waters of the wind in the pine trees."[1] (Agnes Sanford)

In my student days at Seattle Pacific University, I had the good fortune of having a survey class on "the work of the Holy Spirit in the bible." Dr. Wayne McCowan, the Greek language professor, taught the class. Each student was required to keep a large three-ring binder of notes on the Holy Spirit from Genesis to Revelation, 66 books of the bible. We studied the passages for Spirit in Hebrew, *ruach*, and in Greek, *pneuma*. This study lasted the entire quarter, 12 weeks of class.

Toward the end of the class, Dr. McCowan gave us his ideas on the "filling or release of the Holy Spirit" in a Christian's life. His explanation with an illustration was very helpful to me. He took a rubber balloon and blew his breath into it. He then tied a knot in the neck of the balloon to contain the air. He said, "This is the Christian life when a person receives Jesus as their Lord and Savior, and the Holy Spirit comes to live inside him or her." Next, he took the balloon and tossed it in the air and blew upon it, making it move in the air currents. As we watched the balloon float through the air, he said, "This is the person that is filled with the Holy Spirit and is immersed in the power of God." The biblical text for this truth is John 20:22 when Jesus breathed on the disciples and said, "Receive the Holy Spirit." This action by Jesus was in preparation for the Pentecost celebration, which occurred fifty days after Easter and the Lord's resurrection from death.

In the New Testament books of Acts written by Luke; St. Paul's letters to the Ephesians, Galatians, and Romans; and in the apostle

---

[1] Agnes Sanford, *The Healing Gifts of the Spirit* (New York: Harper Collins, 1984), 23.

John's gospel and letters, to be filled with the Holy Spirit was a second work of grace. It was an immediate action by Jesus in sending and/or immersing the believers in the Holy Spirit. This was my experience as well. In the book of Acts, there are seven "fillings of the Holy Spirit:" Acts 2:4; Acts 4:31; Acts 7:54-56 (Stephen, the first martyr); Acts 9:17 (Saul becomes Paul and is filled with the Holy Spirit); Acts 10:44-47 (Gentiles); Acts 11:15-16 (Peter preaching and the Gentiles baptized with the Holy Spirit); and Acts 19:2-7 (Paul preaching to 12 men in Ephesus, laying on hands, and the "Holy Spirit came upon them and they spoke in tongues").

In the last account of the 12 men in Ephesus receiving the Holy Spirit, they had not heard of Jesus but only John's baptism unto repentance for sins. They had not heard of Jesus as baptizer in the Holy Spirit.[2] When Paul explained that Jesus was the one to come after John the Baptist and that the Holy Spirit was sent by Jesus to live in each believer, they were all filled with the Spirit and began to prophesy and to speak in tongues. Paul stayed in Ephesus for two years preaching the Word of Jesus and teaching the disciples about the Holy Spirit. The church was a charismatic congregation utilizing the gifts of the Holy Spirit to heal the sick, cast out demons, prophesy, and preach the Gospel of Christ utilizing "signs and wonders." The Ephesian church lasted until 262 A.D when the Goths destroyed the city. Paul wrote the epistle to Ephesians from Rome in 61 A.D, shortly before his death in 66 A.D.

Paul's teaching on the Holy Spirit followed his own experience in Damascus when Ananias laid hands on him and, his eyesight was healed, and he was filled with the Holy Spirit. He had already believed in Jesus as Lord because he had seen him in a vision when he was struck blind. Paul fasted, prayed, and asked Jesus for forgiveness for his sins of murder, hatred toward God, pride, and disbelief.

Paul already knew the risen Lord Jesus Christ. He had seen a vision from God of Ananias coming to pray for him. Jesus sent the Holy Spirit to fill Paul, and he began to preach in Damascus so effectively

---

[2] Acts 19:2.

that it was necessary for him to escape from the city out a window lowered in a basket in the middle of the night because of death threats.

From there, Paul went to live in the Syrian Desert for three years. I believe it was during this time that Paul had his "great rapture into the third heaven."[3] When Paul says he knew a man 14 years ago, he is speaking of himself. This letter was written around 56 A.D, so Paul would be reflecting on a mystical experience that he had around 42 AD, which would fit the chronology of his time in the desert.[4]

I was filled by the Holy Spirit in November and December of 1971, three weeks after my conversion to Christ at Western Michigan University. This was not a psychological experience in which I believed by faith that I was filled. It was an experience like in Acts 2 with a mighty wind (roar) and fire and praying to God in an unknown language. The only difference was that no one laid hands on me in prayer. I had never heard of the "Baptism of the Spirit" before this event, and I knew no Christians on the campus. I felt my soul-spirit carried away by the Holy Spirit beyond space and time. I refer to this as a mystical experience such as St. Teresa recorded in her book, *Interior Castle.* I also believe it was a baptism by Jesus into the Holy Spirit.

The Ephesian church began with 12 men being filled with the Spirit of God. St Paul told them we are "to be filled with the Spirit." [5]The word in Koine Greek for filled is plerousthe, which means "the habitual and continuing action." It is in the imperative tense, making it a command or order.[6] Paul is contrasting the filling of the Holy Spirit to the Dionysius celebrations wherein the worshipers were indwelt and controlled by the pagan god and given special powers and abilities. For the Christian, the idea is to be controlled by the Spirit and not be ecstatic, but rather to be indwelt by the Spirit of Jesus:

---

[3] 2 Cor. 12:1-5.

[4] The ESV study bible lists Paul's conversion in 33-34 AD and Paul's ministry in the desert (Syria/Cilicia) from 37-45 AD) Crossway pub. ESV study bible, p.2424

[5] Eph. 5:18.

[6] Fritz Rienecker and Cleon L. Rogers, *Linguistic Key to the Greek New Testament* (Grand Rapids: Zondervan, 1982), 538.

"The idea of the word is 'control.' The indwelling Spirit of God is the one who should continually control and dominate the life of the believer. This stands in marked contrast to the worshipers of Dionysius. The present tense calls for a habitual and continuing action. The passive could be permissive passive, 'allow yourselves to be ...'"[7]

The Believer must ask by prayer to receive the filling of the Holy Spirit. When the Holy Spirit comes upon a person, he or she knows it. There are physical manifestations. Jesus breaks into our time and space, and we feel inebriated by the Spirit of God. In his prayer for the Ephesian church, Paul writes, "... and to know this love that surpasses knowledge-that you may be filled to the measure of all the fullness of God."[7] [8]

The word filled is in the aorist passive tense, which means it was an action in the past to be repeated in the present. The same word for fill in Greek is used when Paul prays this prayer: "... and God placed all things under his feet and appointed him to be head over everything for the church, which is his body, the fullness of him who fills everything in every way."[9] The word is a participle and means is *filling* in the transitive, active-passive tense, *pleroumenou*.

The question is why has not the church taught the laou tou Theou (*people of God*) this truth? I believe that Satan has brought confusion into the teaching of the church on the "Fullness of the Holy Spirit." Pastors are afraid to teach this truth to the people feeling that some might object and withhold their financial support or, worst of all, leave the church. But the main reason for our lack of power and gifts of the Holy Spirit is because average Christians want to be comfortable and are unwilling to surrender their whole body, soul, and mind to Jesus Christ as Lord.

The bible has become the Holy Spirit for many Christians. By this, I mean that they think that in reading the bible they have received the

---

[7] *Ibid.*

[8] Eph. 3:19 NIV.

[9] Eph. 1:22-23 NIV.

Spirit.[10] The Pharisees in Jesus' day did this, and he rebuked them when he said, "You search the scriptures because you think that in them you have eternal life; but it is they that bear witness to me, yet you refuse to come to me that you may have life."[11]

In his book *The Gift of the Holy Spirit Today,* Dr. J. Rodman Williams wrote the following regarding miracles and signs and wonders:

"It is a serious error indeed to relegate miracles to the past. It is pathetic to hear among those who vigorously affirm the message of salvation--the necessity of regeneration--that 'signs and wonders' are not to be expected any longer .... Let us say further that it makes little practical difference whether one affirms that the miracles in Acts (or elsewhere) are simply legendary accretions to the record-and thus really did not happen-or that they did happen but no longer occur in our time. Both views deny the reality of the living God who is always free and able in any time to perform His extraordinary works through men. The 'Bible believer' who affirms that miracles were for then but not for now is actually farther removed from a living faith than the 'liberal' who has not gone so far as to lock the power of God into past history. Both, however, need to hear the words of Jesus, 'Is not this why you are wrong, that you know neither the scriptures nor the power of God.'[12]"[13]

My experience in a conservative Christian university and a liberal theological seminary affirms what Dr. Williams has written. The most shocking truth was that the liberal professors did not read, study, or know the scholarly evangelical books on theology. They were only "talking heads" for views learned at Harvard and Yale. The one exception to this was Dr. Lamin Sanneh of Yale University, who gave

---

[10] Tozer, 15. ("It assumes, for instance, that if we have the word for a thing, we have the thing itself. If it is in the bible, it is in us. If we have the doctrine, we have the experience.")

[11] John 5:39-40 ESV.

[12] Mark 12:24.

[13] J. Rodman Williams, *The Gift of the Holy Spirit Today*, (Plainfield: Logos International, 1980), 59.

a week-long series of talks at San Francisco Theological Seminary. He was introduced as the "second Augustine," which immediately got my attention. Dr. Sanneh told the professors, students, and guests that it was a mistake to avoid teaching from Romans and Pauline theology, i.e., "justification by faith." In his letter to the Romans, Paul states, "Therefore, since we have been justified by faith, we have peace with God through our Lord Jesus Christ."[14] Lamin Sanneh was the only professor that ever mentioned Pauline theology in my three years at the seminary. He actually discussed the great doctrine of "justification by faith."[15] Though he was the son of an African tribal chief and a convert from Islam, no one said a word to him about his lectures on mission and World Christianity. At Yale, he was the D. Willis James Professor of Missions and World Christianity Professor of History.

The great tragedy of the church in America today is that it is powerless, lukewarm, and indecisive. The shepherds spend little time in prayer and a great deal of time in corporate planning and fund-raising. How different it was for A. W. Tozer, who would spend two hours every afternoon in his study praying with his body prostrate on the floor. Rev. Tozer would see no visitors in his church office in Chicago between the hours of 1:00 and 3:00. He was a man of prayer and a prophet who never attended a bible college or seminary. He was filled with the Holy Spirit and walked in the power of God. Tozer was highly critical of the evangelical church in America in the 1950s and 1960s. He believed that the church was using the advertising and entertainment strategies of Madison Avenue in New York to cause church growth instead of empowerment by the Holy Spirit.

While reading Tozer's sermons, I came upon the account of John Tollar, a disciple of Meister Eckhart and a great pre-reformation preacher in Germany, and Nicholas, the farmer who implored the great preacher to speak on the subject of the "deeper Christian life." The pastor preached a 22-point sermon on the subject. After the sermon, the peasant farmer Nicholas said the following to Toller:

---

[14] Rom. 5:1.
[15] Rom. 3:23-24.

"'...but I discern that you were preaching it to others as truth without having experienced the implication of deep spiritual principles in your own life!' Nicholas told him, 'You are not living in full identification with the death and resurrection of Jesus Christ. I could tell by the way you preached ... I could tell!'"[16]

Tozer went on to say that the great preacher stopped preaching for a season seeking the illumination of the Holy Spirit renewal in his life. Finally, after a "long period of dark sufferings in his soul," Tollar experienced the Holy Spirit falling upon him. Tozer describes it in his sermon:

"The great flood of the Spirit came in on his life, and he returned to his parish and to his pulpit to become one of the greatest and most fervent and effective preachers of his generation. God's gracious blessings came, but Tollar first had to die. This is what Paul meant when he said, 'I have been crucified with Christ.'"[17]

Jeremiah, the weeping prophet of God, was just a teenager when he was called away from farming to be a prophet to Judah in the 6th century BC. He was not popular because he prophesied that Babylon would destroy the nation and take the people of Judah away in captivity because they were idolatrous and rebellious. Much of what Jeremiah preached to the people in his day parallels America in the twenty-first century:

"For the shepherds have become dull-hearted, and have not sought the Lord; therefore, they shall not prosper, and all their flocks shall be scattered ... O Lord, I know the way of man is not in himself; it is not in man who walks to direct his own steps. 0 Lord, correct me, but not in your anger, lest you bring me to nothing."[18]

When Jane and I were ministering in the ghetto of the Irish Channel in New Orleans, we were reading Dr. J. Rodman Williams's book on the Holy Spirit. It gave us a compass to go by on the sea of

[16] A. W. Tozer, The Tozer Pulpit, vol. 2, ed. Gerald B. Smith (Camp Hill:Christian Publications, 1994), 134.

[17] *Ibid.*

[18] Jer. 10:22, 23-24.

adversity that we were navigating. We preached and taught that signs and wonders were for today and that the Holy Spirit and the word of prophecy (word of knowledge) were available to all who call upon the name of Jesus in sincerity and surrender fully to the Lord.

In May of 1975, Dr. Williams had attended a worldwide gathering of 10,000 charismatics in Rome at St. Peter's Basilica in the Vatican. An extraordinary prophecy was given which I believe has yet to be fulfilled but may soon come to pass in America and the world;

> "My people, I speak to you of a new day. I speak to you of the dawning of a new age in my church. I speak to you of a day that has not been seen before, of a life on the earth not seen before in my church. Prepare yourselves for me. Prepare yourselves for the action I begin now, because the things you see around you will change.
>
> "The combat you must enter into now is different, it is new. You need wisdom from me you do not have now. You need the power of my Holy Spirit in a way you have not possessed before! You need an understanding of my will and of the way I work that you do not have now. Open your eyes, open your hearts, prepare yourselves for me and for the day I announce now. My church will be different, my people will be different. Difficulty and trial will come upon you. Comfort that you know now will be far from you. But the comfort you will have is the comfort of my Holy Spirit. They will seek for you to take your life, but I will support you! Come to me. Bind yourselves together around me because I proclaim a new day of victory and triumph for your God. Behold it is begun!"[19]

This prophetic word from Rome is now forty years old, but I believe that it is from the Holy Spirit and is for today. If we are living in the "last days," then the church will experience persecution from the antichrist, though the church has already conquered the devil who was thrown out of heaven:

> "Now the salvation and the power and the kingdom of our God and the authority of his Christ have come, for the accuser of our

---

[19] Williams, 56.

brothers has been thrown down, who accuses them day and night before our God. And they have conquered him by the blood of the Lamb and by the word of their testimony, for they loved not their lives even unto death. Therefore, "rejoice O heavens and you who dwell in them! But woe to you, O earth and sea, for the devil has come down to you in great wrath, because he knows his time is short!'"[20]

In 1921, Paul Rader wrote the hymn, "We Are Gathered for Thy Blessing." Beneath the title of the song is a text from the bible: "My message and my preaching were ... with a demonstration of the Spirit's power."[21] I especially like this old hymn because it emphasizes waiting on God in prayer as John Tollar did. It tells of grace and the blood of Jesus for salvation and the promise of the Holy Ghost and Fire for Christians for power to serve Christ:

1. We are gathered for thy blessing, we will wait upon our God; We will trust in Him who loved us, and who bought us with His blood.
2. We will glory in the power, we will sing of wondrous grace; In our midst as thou hast promised, Come, O come and take thy place.
3. Bring us low in prayer before Thee, and with faith our souls inspire, 'til we claim by faith the promise of the Holy Ghost and fire.

Refrain: Spirit now melts and move all of
  our hearts with love.
  Breathe on us from above with old-
  time power. Amen[22]

---

[20] Rev. 12:10-12 ESV.

[21] 1 Cor. 2:4.

[22] *The Hymnal for Worship and Celebration*, #258 (Waco: Word Music).

My prayer for you as you read these words is that, no matter where you are in life, you may humble yourself so that "in due time Christ may exalt you." As the evangelist Dwight Moody would say to people who questioned why we needed the Holy Spirit after we are already Christians, "We need the Holy Spirit again and again because we leak."[23]

---

[23] Most Evangelicals agree that the Holy Spirit is needed for mission work and to overcome our old, carnal natures. However, the Evangelicals deny that the "sign-gifts," like prophecy, discernment of evil spirits, speaking in tongues, and healing are for today. They believe that the charismatic gifts ended when the last apostle died. This is the teaching of Dispensationalism from John Nelson Darby and the Plymouth Brethren.

XIV
The *KABOD* – Glory of God

"... and the Word became flesh and dwelt among us, and we beheld his glory as of the only begotten of the Father, full of grace and truth." (John 1:14 NKJ)

Jane had a great dream in which she saw the condition of the church in America. In my journal dated November 27, 1984, I wrote the following:

"Jane had a 'great dream' last night! In the dream, we were in our car driving to Portland, Oregon, from Seattle, Washington. The freeway, Interstate 5, was in complete devastation with bridges and roadways destroyed. I got lost driving the car as nothing looked familiar. Jane fell asleep as we drove through the maze of broken concrete and cars strewn about like toys. Finally, in my desperation to find our way, I pulled the car off the road down to a flat, grassy area that was quite well maintained. A large rectangular swimming pool was in front of us with a gardener filling the crystal clear, blue water pool with a fire hose. A great volume of water was streaming out of the hose under great pressure, and Jane was afraid we might get hit by the water! Surrounding the pool were neatly dug furrows for vegetables with strings above the rows. But there was no growth yet as the plants had not germinated!"

I asked Jane what she thought the dream meant, and she replied, "The dream has to do with the great chaos of destruction that Satan has caused in the world. This is spiritual warfare. The gardener or caretaker represents pastors in the church who are trying to control the Holy Spirit, which is the rushing water. The garden that has not borne any fruit, but has great potential, is the church in America."

This dream had come exactly one year after a prophecy that I gave to the San Mateo church at a Friday night Prayer and Praise meeting on November 27, 1983. I gave the pastor of the church, Rev. Pitman, the following transcript of the prophecy:

"To the leaders of the church say: the evil one, Satan, will come upon you this year like a flood! You will be unable to resist him in your own strength or training! But know this, I stand in your midst, and I am raising a standard against the flood of evil. Your faith will be sorely tested by this trial. Do not attempt to resist the enemy in your own strength or power! You must rely upon me, and do not be surprised when these things come to pass for, I have warned you by my word, and it shall come to pass this next year!"

After I gave this strong word from the Lord with a specific time reference, two women from the church confirmed the word. One woman was an elder, and the other woman was the pastor's wife, Marilyn Pitman. A week later, after reading my prophecy regarding the church, my mentor, Robert Pitman, said, "I don't believe this is from the Lord!" My feelings were not hurt at all, because I knew it was God speaking, and it had been confirmed by two witnesses who were Godly women. Many other people at the meeting knew it was from the Holy Spirit as well. We all wondered what kind of attack the demons were planning, especially since this church was the only one in the entire area of the Mid-Peninsula Bay Area that was doing deliverance ministry and casting out of demons on a regular basis. Furthermore, the San Mateo Police Department was sending us all the demoniacs in the area, because of Rev. Pitman's relationship with them as chaplain of the police department. Why this prophecy so unsettled the church is still a mystery to me. It was very predictable that Satan would try to shut down the church through conflict or scandal.

The first test case was one of the members of Prayer and Praise, Bonnie. She had been having trouble with her husband, a college professor. He was very abusive, both physically and verbally. Bonnie had sought counseling in the church to no avail. She turned to Jane and me for help, and we advised her to leave her dangerous domestic situation. Bonnie had nowhere to go, so I called John Sandford of Elijah House Ministries. I had read John and Paula Sandford's book, *The Elijah Task*, and had greatly benefited from it. He agreed to shelter Bonnie and her daughter, Heather.

The members of the church staff were upset with Jane and me for helping the mother and daughter. The counseling given to Bonnie had been of no help, and she was in danger. Matters worsened, because we refused to tell anyone, including the senior minister, where Bonnie had gone.

The Sandford's helped Bonnie and her daughter get healing for wounded memories. They also gave her work typing a manuscript for another book, *Transformation of the Inner Man*. John and Paula had begun working with Agnes Sanford in 1963 in the School of Pastoral Care. They were teaching about "healing of the inner man." John came to see that the blood of Jesus deals with our sin by forgiveness, but the death on the cross requires our participation daily to overcome our old sin nature. While typing this manuscript, Bonnie was healed of her memories of 20 years of abuse. In chapter one, she read the following passage, which contains the essence of the book:

> "These ministers seemed to me like gardeners continually lopping off weeds which just as persistently regrew from the roots. None seemed to comprehend the whole job, to lay the ax to the roots. Roots lie hidden, beneath the surface. Neither healers nor pastors seemed to know how to transform our carnal natures at the deep level of causes, dealing both with sins and the sin nature. This I foresaw as the great lack in the Church, and therefore an explanation for the continuing lack of maturity through lack of true sanctification and transformation in the Body of Christ."[1]

Bonnie and her daughter stayed a year at Elijah House Ministries. She had her own apartment and worked odd jobs. Bonnie wrote me a letter on November 24, 1984, which read, "Mike, you can relax before God and know your advice to us was right on! ... Well, I will close and help Paula with dinner. I thank you for all your love, prayers, and practical assistance. I know you will reap in joy."

---

[1] John and Paula Sandford, *The Transformation of the Inner Man* (Plainfield: Bridge Publishing, 1982), 5.

On Wednesday, February 22, 1984, Jane and I had a meeting with Dolores Winder,[2] who was doing a healing conference at the Presbyterian Church. An elder, Paul Linquist, had called me at midnight and suggested that I make an appointment with Mrs. Winder to get prayer and wisdom for my pastoral vocation. At this meeting, I explained to her that I had been seeking a "call of God" for four years and that I thought I might be experiencing demonic opposition. Mrs. Winder told Jane and me that "God doesn't tempt us with evil for four years without giving us grace. God has protected you from a trap." She explained that if we had gotten into a Presbyterian church, they would have stifled our gifts and put too many controls on us. Instead, God has protected us by shutting the doors. She said we should look further afield and broaden our horizons beyond denominations and think about using our gifts for teaching and deliverance ministry in a wider spectrum.[3]

This prophetess and healer went on to say that God would lift the spirit of heaviness" from me and clean me out by the Holy Spirit. She said she saw "streams of water flowing from me and touching many other people." After the powerful prayer, I felt dizzy and giddy for five hours. I began to praise the Lord Jesus for this word of wisdom to me and a new sense of relief and freedom. I know that the enemy lays "traps," "snares," "gins," and "nets" as King David sings in Psalms 140 and 141.[4] David would rejoice in God the Lord as the "strength of my salvation."

A number of people were healed and overwhelmed by the Holy Spirit in Dolores and Bill Winder's ministry among us at the Presbyterian Church. Bonnie had a dream on the night before the prayer and healing meeting, which I recorded in my journal:

"We had several men catch people as they went down under the power of the Holy Spirit. As we worshiped and praised the Lord

[2] "God's miraculous healing of Dolores Winder was one of the great miracles of the Twentieth Century. Her ministry is like walking again through the pages of the Book of Acts." Bill Keith

[3] M.S. Lynch, *Journal*, Feb. 22, 1984.

[4] Pss. 140:5, 141:9-10.

in prayer and praise, the Lord Jesus told us through prophecy to 'put on the gifts' and do not be unclothed. Bonnie told us of a dream she had the night before. She went to a Christmas party but was not dressed properly. The Christmas tree was bare, and the decorations were all in paper bags on the floor. God told her that we need to 'use the gifts of the Spirit to build up the body of Christ and produce the fruit of righteousness!'"[5]

After we left the Presbyterian Church, we felt sad and missed the fellowship of our friends. Yet the Holy Spirit was leading us to begin to meet with other churches and expand our vision of the Kingdom of God. For a while we attended Carlmont Christian Center in San Carlos. There we heard a very interesting sermon on the prophets Joel, Isaiah, and Jeremiah, given by the Rev. Charles Gaines:

"There have been three distinct movements of the Holy Spirit in the last 500 years. The first was releasing the Word of God in the Reformation by Martin Luther; the second was the Charismatic movement on fruitless churches. This was an act of grace on the part of God and stayed his hand of judgment. It was laity-led from person to person and church to church. The third movement of the Holy Spirit will be different from the Charismatic movement because God will be raising up leaders and churches of 'deep teaching and storehouses.' (Pastor Gaines omitted the first and second Great Awakenings, which I would have included!)

"God's *kabod--glory* will fall from heaven in great power and will usher in the Millennial Kingdom (Rev. 20: The angel binds Satan for 1,000 years). It will be a time of great spiritual power, signs and wonders that will be unprecedented. There will also be judgment on the fig trees that do not bear fruit. The pastor said there will be a violence about this Kingdom as God rips out the unrighteousness, and 'forceful men will lay hold of it.'[6] This will be known as the DAY OF THE LORD!"[7]

---

[5] M.S. Lynch, Journal, Feb. 25, 1984.

[6] Matt. 11:12 KJV.

[7] M.S. Lynch, Journal, Dec. 23, 1984.

XV
Tidal Wave of Mud Dream

"Life without possibility of parole is like a slow, prolonged death of body, spirit, and soul." (Tony Wimberly, Mule Creek State Prison)

A loud clanging noise outside my house sent me to the door to determine what was causing all the commotion. A large, orange, dump truck was backing into my driveway. When I opened the door to shout at the driver, I saw a massive 100-foot tidal wave of mud heading toward my house. A young woman and her child were walking on the sidewalk in front of my house. I yelled out to her, "Don't resist the mud or you will die! Instead, swim on top of it and you will live!" In an instant, we were all swept away, the woman, her small child, and I. We swam on top of the mud for what seemed like a long time. Gradually, the mud subsided as it rolled into the high Sierra Mountains. We walked out of the mud unharmed and into the tall pines that were like a refuge. The sun was shining through the trees, and the birds were singing. We were safe!

This was a vision I had upon waking in 1985, three years before beginning my chaplaincy at the Alameda County Sheriff's Department on April 4, 1988. The dream turned out to be quite prophetic in my life and that of my family. I was the first chaplain hired by Alameda County in many years. My assignment was to work at North County Jail in Oakland plus the inherited position at the Santa Rita Jail in Dublin. Santa Rita was named after the patron saint of the poor and outcast. She was patroness of impossible causes and broken hearted women.

Jane cried when I told her that my long sojourn to find my place as a minister had ended. My daughter Monika was three years old, and we had a new baby, Chloe, born in July of 1989. We moved to Tracy, a sleepy farming community on the other side of the Altamont Hills in San Joaquin County.

After hearing the news that I finally had a good job and vocation, our close friends, Rick and Marie, invited us to their home for dinner. They were both successful lawyers and could afford to buy a house in San Carlos. They were involved at First Presbyterian Church in San Mateo. After dinner, the couple asked if they could lay hands on us and pray for our new adventure in the jails. It was Easter weekend, and we were celebrating life. As we prayed, Marie's strange friend began to prophesy saying, "Be careful in your new job. I see a man with a large swollen head that looks like an orange. He oozes with sweetness on the outside, but inside the man is a ravenous wolf." This was not the type of blessing I was expecting, but knowing Marie and her walk with God, I wrote it in my journal and thought about the warning. Jane has always remembered the prophetess "word of knowledge" and would remind me of it when I experienced great opposition in my work as chaplain in the jails, "the tidal wave of mud" and the "orange man."

The first minister I invited to visit the jail and have lunch with me was my mentor, Robert Pitman. He was the chaplain for the San Mateo Police Department and was eager to see the jail in Oakland. I took him to the best seafood restaurant in Jack London Square, just four blocks from North County Jail. We ate at Scott's Seafood Grill on the waterfront, and I picked up the bill. That was a first. Bob Pitman had always paid the bills when I was with him.

Bob had originally encouraged me to be a police chaplain like him, but since few are paid a salary, I did not want another volunteer job. My job with Alameda County was a management position with cafeteria benefits and a pension. My salary enabled Jane and me to buy our first house and to have good medical insurance. The commute from Tracy to Oakland was only 50 minutes at that time, and I would listen to preachers like David Jeremiah and Jack Hayford during the drive.

Deacon Frank Beville from Catholic Charities worked with me at NCJ and Santa Rita. Frank was a Catholic charismatic deacon and a very good counselor with many gifts of the Spirit. He had the gift of discernment of spirits and could tell if an inmate was demonized or just mentally ill or both. Frank was an older, counter-culture man who wore Birkenstocks to work and was very low key. A major heart attack had caused him to reevaluate his life and led to him being filled with the Holy Spirit and an ordained deacon.

After being at the downtown jail for three months, I learned that the Lutheran chaplain at Santa Rita had died after a long battle with cancer. I was told by Captain Hickerson that I would need to handle both jails, coordinate all religious activities, and counsel more than 3,000 inmates. I asked the good captain how I was to do all this by myself. He said, "Split your time between the two jails and work out your own schedule." So, I did. Frank and I emptied out the old storeroom of bibles and Christian literature in four days. We called upon trustee inmates to take the bibles to all the units in the jail. The prisoners, who were predominantly African-American and Hispanic, were hungry and thirsty for the Word of God and reacted like it was Christmas. Our chapel services were packed, and inmates had to be turned away from services. The Holy Spirit was convicting men and women of their need for Jesus as their Savior and King. Many lives were transformed. Between the two jails, about 800 religious volunteers came in at least once a month. More than 65,000 men and women prisoners passed through these two Alameda County jails in a year. This revival, or "Golden Age" as Frank Beville called it, lasted from 1988 to 1992.[1]

The Rev. Glen Morrison of Follow Up Ministries had trained many of the volunteers at both jails. He had bible studies that the inmates would send through the mail. They would be graded and sent back to the inmates with a new series of studies. I videotaped my sermons and broadcast them at both jails on Sunday so that even those inmates who could not attend chapel could hear the Gospel. This was especially important to those in "administrative segregation." These inmates did not mix with others and were allowed out of their cells only 45 minutes each day.

---

[1] Matt du Plessis, son of the famous Pentecostal minister David du Plessis, lived in Oakland. Matt had gathered four other ministers to pray for me at his house during the first week of my chaplaincy. The Holy Spirit honored their prayers for a revival among the convicts in the jails in an amazing way.

In all my years working as a chaplain in the jails, I never had one incident with an inmate or ever feared for my life. The angels of the Lord were there, and I was given unusual grace to minister to inmates in the Holy Spirit and power. But the jail administration was a different story. They saw corrections as punitive and not as opportunities to rehabilitate men and women. That is why I opposed the death penalty.

One of the first inmates I met, courtesy of Rev. Glen Morrison, was Anthony Wimberly. Tony was only 22 years old when I met him in 1988. He was facing the death penalty for three random murders of women in Oakland and the rape of a 12 year-old child, who survived even after being shot. In the system's eyes, Tony was "human garbage," the term often used by the Sheriff when referring to the prisoners. But in God's eyes, which are the only ones that count, they are seen as lost sheep valuable to the Lord. In Jesus' first sermon, he used a text from Isaiah to proclaim the "year of the Lord's favor":

> "The Spirit of the Lord God is upon me, because the Lord has anointed me to bring good news to the poor; he has sent me to bind up the brokenhearted, to proclaim liberty to the captives, and the opening of the prison to those who are bound; to proclaim the year of the Lord's favor, and the day of vengeance of our God ...."[2]

The prophet Isaiah told the chosen people of Israel that they were to be "a light to the nations." He described their covenant with God Almighty to be this:

> "...to open the eyes that are blind, to bring out the prisoners from the dungeon, from the prison those who sit in darkness. I am the Lord; that is my name; my glory I give to no other, nor my praise to carved idols. Behold, the former things have come to pass, and new things I now declare; before they spring forth I tell you of them."[3]

To say that prisoners are "garbage" or the "scum of the earth" is to violate the covenant of God made by Jesus Christ on the cross for all people. Isaiah prophesied from 740 BC until about 680 BC. Jesus chose this prophet to quote because Jesus himself fulfilled those prophecies

[2] Isa. 61:1-2 ESV.

[3] Isa. 42:7-9 ESV.

by healing the blind, raising the dead, providing hope to the despised, and giving the Holy Spirit to all who believe in him as the Messiah. Isaiah prophesied that the Redeemer would come in power:

"So they shall fear the name of the Lord from the west, and his glory from the rising of the sun; for he will come like a 'rushing stream, which the wind of the Lord drives. And a redeemer will come to Zion, to those in Jacob who turn from transgression,' declares the Lord."[4]

Tony Wimberly was one of those murderers who turned from his wicked ways and repented of his sins. When I met him in April of 1988, he had already been at North County Jail for several years. Rev. Glen Morrison was doing bible study with Tony on Sunday mornings. I sat in the multipurpose room with Glen and Tony, and I saw a prisoner facing the death penalty with peace and purpose in his fractured life. Glen and I baptized Tony after his sentencing was completed. We testified as subpoenaed character witnesses in Tony's three death penalty trials. The first two trials were 11-1 verdicts. A death penalty verdict must be unanimous. In both trials, one lone juror could not vote for death. In both trials, a Christian followed her conscience and could not vote for Tony's death despite enormous pressure to do so. In the third trial, because there were enough mitigating circumstances to override this extreme punishment, the verdict was 8-4.

Alameda County spent three million dollars on these three trials, and the politicians were not happy with the outcome. So, they decided to go after the chaplain who testified on behalf of the inmate, Tony Wimberly... me, Glen was not a county employee.

The Alameda Sheriff's Department went on a witch hunt with me as their prey. I had testified on behalf of five inmates facing the death penalty. In all these cases, I was subpoenaed by the defense attorneys, which meant I was required to appear before the court. I was happy to tell the truth regarding the prisoners that I knew from North County Jail. I had worked with all of them in Sunday services one-on-one because they were in isolation, "administrative segregation," due to

---

[4] Isa. 59:19-20 ESV.

the nature of their crimes. The Sheriff's department initiated three internal affairs investigations of me from 1993 until my termination on February 4,1998. They tried to discharge me so that I would not be available to testify on behalf of other inmates facing the death penalty. Since I was a member of Local 3 of the S.E.I.U union. I was afforded legal protection, and attorneys to represent me.

In the first internal affairs action, I was investigated and put on "leave with pay." It began in November and lasted about eight weeks. The Sheriff's department dropped it because no evidence of wrongdoing was found. Usually it is unknown who causes internal affairs investigations. That is a secret. But the charges against me were given in writing, and they were completely manufactured. This first investigation was instigated by a new inmate services director named Charles. He alleged that I received 20 dollars from an inmate and spent it. In truth, I put the check in the bank for the inmate, and I had the receipt. This new employee was eventually terminated, but he caused Frank Beville and me many problems.

On February 4, 1992, I wrote in my journal:

"I am having a quiet time of prayer and meditation. In my sorrow at leaving Santa Rita Jail as the chaplain, I sought the Lord and He reminded me of Psalm 71:19-21: 'Your righteousness reaches to the skies, O God, You who have done great things. Who, O God, is like you? Though you have made me see troubles, many and bitter, you will restore my life again; from the depths of the earth you will again bring me up. You will increase my honor and comfort me once again.'[5]"

After being transferred back to North County Jail in Oakland, I was asked to speak at a Full Gospel Businessman's meeting. A woman whom I did not know came up to me and gave me this word of knowledge from the Lord: "You have a broken and contrite spirit and God will honor this and bless you in your ministry. We are in the last days, and God is refining the church with fire, and Satan is very active as he knows his days are short." Lou May then said, "You

---

[5] Ps. 71:19-21 NIV.

are fighting demonic strongholds, and they can only be pulled down through prayer."[6] I knew that there were strong territorial spirits over Oakland and that my fight was not with man but with the "powers and authorities"[7] "for we wrestle not against flesh...."[8]

Once the charges were dropped, I returned to work and was again commuting an hour each way between Tracy and Oakland. Jane and I had bought a house in Tracy because it was only a 25 minute commute on highway 580 to Santa Rita. The inmate services director meant it for evil, but God meant it for good. I was reunited with all the prisoners facing the death penalty, and I could renew my fellowship with some of them. Since this downtown jail had only 920 inmates, it was easier for me to see more of them.

At the North County Jail, the religious volunteers were exceptional. Priscilla and Terry Allen were two of these special people. They had the gift of prophecy and were filled with the Holy Spirit. Priscilla was an ordained minister, and Terry was a steelworker. They were several years older than me, and I benefited from and enjoyed their fruitful ministry among the inmates. After the bible study on December 30, 1996, we had a time of prayer in the conference room next to my office, and I prayed for healing for some of the volunteers. The Holy Spirit fell upon all 12 of us and refreshed us with the "Balm of Gilead," anointing us with the oil of the Holy Spirit. After this powerful time of prayer and anointing by God, I talked with Terry and Priscilla for an hour. Terry said to me, "I have a word from the Book of Isaiah for you in your time of affliction and persecution:

"Don't be afraid. I am with you. Don't tremble with fear. I am your God. I will make you strong, as I protect you with my arm and give you victories. Everyone who hates you will be terribly disgraced; those who attack will vanish into thin air. You will look around for those brutal enemies, but you won't find them because they will be

---

[6] M.S. Lynch, Journal, February, 1992.

[7] Col. 2:15.

[8] Eph. 6:10-12.

gone. I am the Lord your God. I am holding your hand, so don't be afraid. I am here to help you."[9]

I needed to apply this Word of God to my life as a *Rhema* Word (a personal prophetic word meant for me), because a second internal affairs investigation had begun in October of 1996. On November 14, 1996, I testified in the fifth death penalty case involving Michael Ihde. Michael had become a Christian and was a regular in our one-on-one services at NCJ. As I testified as to Michael's change in character after receiving Jesus Christ, three members of Internal Affairs sat in the front row in plain clothes taking notes. It was an obvious attempt by them to intimidate me from testifying as a character witness subpoenaed by the public defender, Judy Brown.

During a recess in the trial, I informed Ms. Brown that the Internal Affairs deputies were sitting in the front row of the court taking notes. This was highly unusual. To get it into the record, Ms. Brown asked me, "Chaplain, are you afraid of losing your job because of your testimony here in this death penalty trial?" I replied, "Yes." Then Ms. Brown asked me, "What is conversion?" I said, "Conversion is a new birth in the Spirit from above that changes a person's mind and heart toward God." I quoted John 3:16, and I said, "Michael is not the same person who killed and raped a woman years ago."

I left the courtroom accompanied by several of my religious volunteers. One of these was Cornelius Cassimere, a large black man who was a longshoreman on the Oakland waterfront and a devout Christian. I felt safe in his company. The Internal Affairs deputies were in the elevator with us. I introduced them to my volunteers, "These are the folks from the Sheriff's Department's Internal Affairs Division." They did not respond, and we all went our separate ways, but I knew then that I had to retain the best attorneys available, because the Union Local 3 was not doing anything for my defense.

I had every reason to believe that the Sheriff's Department was going to try to send me to prison. They filed two charges against me. The first was lying under oath. The second was sending documents, i.e., letters

---

[9] Isa. 41:10-13 CEV.

to the court, without the proper authorization by a supervisor. I started asking my deputy friends who would be the best attorney I could hire. They all said, "Mike Rains. He represents Oakland PD." At my own expense, I hired Michael Rains of Carrol, Burdick, and McDonough law firm to represent me. Mike had the reputation of being a bulldog in legal matters. His associate, Rockne Lucia, represented me as well.

During a four and a half hour taped interview, Mike Rains accused the Internal Affairs captain, Linda Elliot, and Sgt. Knudsen of "harassing the chaplain and depriving him of due process of law." Rains also said that the District Attorney and Internal Affairs were "conspiring to intimidate Chaplain Lynch as a witness in five death penalty trials that he had been subpoenaed to testify on their behalf." He was furious and called the proceedings "asinine." Despite my attorneys' threats of a lawsuit, the Sheriff's Department had refused to turn over 37 letters I had written to Christian book distributors and religious donors who then had sent me free materials. Sgt. Knudsen had confiscated my computer at work and refused to return it, thus denying me "due process," because I had no other record of these letters. In the hearings that followed, every time a letter was introduced into the record, Rockne Lucia and I would have to leave the conference room for a side bar conference. This went on for three months, from October of 1995 to January of 1996. Their attempts to bankrupt me with legal fees of $200 an hour nearly succeeded. But my God "owns the cattle on a thousand hills."[10]

Jane and I had no savings account. We had two small children that Jane stayed at home to care for. I did not know what the outcome of these hearings would be, and I had no idea from where I was going to get $10,000 to pay my legal fees. I felt like I was being crucified with Christ without the resurrection to new life. Looking back at this "dark night of the spirit," I believe that Satan was trying me in the furnace of affliction because of the successes of the Gospel in the prisoners' lives. Referring to his own crucifixion, Jesus said, "If I be lifted up I will draw all men to Myself."[11]

---

[10] Ps. 50:10 NKJ.

[11] John 12:32 NKJ.

Looking back on this experience with the Sheriff's departments Internal Affairs and County Counsel I would not have survived emotionally if it had not been for the grace of Jesus and the prayers of the saints; maybe even Saint Rita!

XVI
Fresh Angels

"Great is the dignity of souls, so great indeed that each of them has an angel assigned for their protection from the moment one is born." St. Jerome[1]

My attorney and I entered the twelfth floor of the Alameda County building overlooking Lake Merritt Oakland. It was January 6, 1997, and the last day of taped hearings in my second Internal Affairs investigation. We knew the IA lawyers would throw everything they had at us today, so I had asked all of my Christian volunteers, my relatives, and Jane's family to pray for me. God's arm is not so short that he cannot save. I was to see the deliverance of the Lord and the hand of God in action.

While going through this crucible with the Internal Affairs officers and these hearings, I remembered what Bob Whittaker, a Spirit-filled minister from southern California, had said at a retreat I attended. "God is merciful, and He is tremendous to those who wait for Him." I had waited on God a long time for this calling to prison ministry, and I knew that the Lord Jesus Christ placed me in the position as chaplain to prisoners. I was not about to shrink back from the pressure of "the world, the flesh, and the devil." At the beginning of my ministry at North County Jail, I wrote in my journal:

"When we are obedient to the Lord in ministry, Jesus blesses us with his power and grace and the joy of the Holy Spirit. When we serve others, Christ fills us with the Holy Spirit and joy, as was the witness of the church in the Book of Acts 4:31, 33: '...and when they prayed, the place in which they gathered together was shaken, and they were all filled with the Holy Spirit and continued to speak the word of God with boldness...And with great power

---

[1] Hugh Pope, *"Guardian Angel," The Catholic Encyclopedia, Vol. 7.*

the apostles were giving their testimony to the resurrection of the Lord Jesus, and great grace was upon them all.'[2]"

As I faced this last and final hearing, I knew that my volunteers were praying for me and my family. I also trusted in this promise from the bible:

"Fear not, I have redeemed you; I have called you by name, you are mine. When you pass through the waters, I will be with you; and through the rivers, they shall not overwhelm you; when you walk through fire, you shall not be burned, for I am the Lord your God, the Holy One of Israel, your Savior."[3]

I believed these promises made to Israel in 700 BC as also applying to me as a child of the New Covenant in Christ's blood. Jesus fulfilled more than 300 prophecies regarding his coming to earth as the suffering servant and the Messiah or Savior of the world. Isaiah 53 described the coming Messiah and his suffering on the cross, a horrible payment for sin. If Jesus was willing to do this for me, then surely, I could bear testimony to the inmates and the authorities and suffer the consequences.

It was a clear, cold, January day as I entered the building, met my attorney, Rockne Lucia, and rode the elevator to the twelfth floor. We had to walk past a clear, glass-enclosed room overlooking the Oakland skyline, where Sheriff Plummer and his top brass were in a meeting. I could not help but think that I was like the prophet Daniel walking into the lion's den. Then I remembered a little gospel hymn my mother had taught me in childhood. "Dare to be a Daniel; dare to stand alone. Dare to have a purpose firm; dare to make it known." It is strange the thoughts one can have as men are about to "rend you asunder."

My Christian volunteers knew that his last day of the hearing would be the hardest. Internal Affairs had not yet presented any damaging evidence of any guilt on my part regarding either the charge of lying or anything in the 37 letters I had written to book publishers. During these five months of hearings, I was still working at NCJ and was

---

[2] Acts 4:31, 33 ESV.

[3] Isa. 43:1-3a ESV.

being upheld by the prayers of the Christian inmates. I had expected persecution for preaching the prophetic word of Jesus, but the ferocious attacks lasting months and years was taking a toll.

Rockne Lucia was now handling my case entirely due to a conflict of interest regarding Mike Rains. Rains had once represented a deputy sheriff who was involved in my hearings. I had confidence in Lucia representing me because he was a practicing Catholic and believed in the work of the chaplaincy among the prisoners. Lucia, on the other hand, was not confident in a positive outcome in these hearings. The verbose district attorney, Baldwin, did not lose cases like mine and often bragged about the fact. Baldwin's face was always cherry red, and he was very aggressive, even hostile, toward me. His displeasure was evident.

The conference room was very plush with San Francisco 49er memorabilia and artifacts all over the room. Signed pictures of Joe Montana and Jerry Rice hung from the walls. At the far end of the 12-foot-long conference table were two black leather bar chairs that were unoccupied. My attorney and I sat at the front end of the conference table on the right-hand side. The county counsel and Sgt. Knudsen sat across from us on the left-hand side. Our tape recorders were turned on and positioned between us like a referee in a prize fight.

As the hearing convened at 9:00 a.m., my wife, Jane, was praying for me as were scores of volunteers. Even my mother was interceding on my behalf from Michigan. The questioning in the morning went as I expected. Sgt. Knudsen fished around for discrepancies in my testimony. At noon, we recessed for an hour-long lunch break. When we resumed, Sgt. Knudsen switched tactics and began to ask me questions about Satan and demons. I thought this was a very strange tactic. It greatly surprised me. His intention was to make me look like a right-wing religious fanatic who was paranoid regarding the supernatural phenomenon. I imagine his strategy was to embarrass me, but just the opposite occurred. I rose to the challenge and "girded my loins" for action.

I began my answer to the sergeant by quoting St. Paul in the sixth chapter of his letter to the Ephesians: "For we do not wrestle against flesh and blood, but against the rulers, against the authorities, against the cosmic powers over this present darkness, against spiritual forces of evil in the heavenly places."[4] I also gave a brief description of Lucifer and his fall from heaven due to his sin of pride in wanting to be worshipped like God, as stated in Isaiah 14 and Ezekiel 28. I said that these "powers and principalities" (fallen angels) have control to a limited degree over nations, cities, and governments. It was at this point in my oration that I first saw them standing near the black leather chairs at the end of the conference table, two mighty angels.

A deafening silence had engulfed the room, as if time had stopped. It caused me to look up. I beheld two very tall angels with long linen robes trimmed in gold down to their ankles. They were smiling at me and radiating the glory of God and his throne. Though I was stunned, I had to continue responding to the diatribe of the Internal Affairs officers. Both angels carried white, stone-like tablets and were recording all the words spoken by pointing at the tablets with their fingers. Their beautiful smiles and radiant auras suggested they had just come from the presence of the *kabod* glory of God. At some point, the angels sat down in the two large leather chairs, smiling and continuing to take notes. I almost laughed out loud. The angels remained in the room for the entire deposition. We adjourned at 5:00 p.m.

One might think that my reaction would have been to stand up and shout, "Glory, Hallelujah!" Under the circumstances, however, I still felt like I had been crucified with Jesus. I felt spiritually and physically eviscerated. This reaction embarrasses me, but I felt that the heavenly angels had never had to suffer like Jesus. How could they empathize with me? On the other hand, their mission was to carry out the orders of the Lord, not to be the Holy Spirit, the Comforter and my Advocate. The angels are messenger spirits sent to Christians to protect us and help us along the way and to do spiritual warfare on our behalf against Satan.

After the session ended, I walked out of the building with Rockne Lucia. I needed to ask him, "Did you sense an abrupt change in the atmosphere of the conference room when Sgt. Knudsen began to

---

[4] Eph. 6:12 ESV.

ask me my thoughts on Satan and his demons?" Rockne said, "Yes. I did notice a profound silence. What was it?" I said, "It was Jesus sending two eight foot tall angels to stand in the room and record notes." My attorney just stared at me, speechless. So, I told him, "Don't be afraid. You just won the case, which you were so worried about. Congratulations!"

I do not know what Rockne thought about my story of the angels, but I would have loved to hear his report to his boss, Mike Rains. Perhaps he told him, "The good chaplain is having hallucinations because of the pressure he is under." Perhaps he said nothing at all, fearing that he too would be seen as too religious or Catholic or something.

I had promised Jane that I would call her as soon as I returned to my office at the North County Jail. When she answered the phone, I had no chance to recount my story. She immediately said to me, "I was praying for you at 9:00 a.m., and I saw a vision of two angels standing in the room where you were having the meeting. They were *fresh angels!*" I asked, "What is a fresh angel?" She replied, "They are the angels that stand in the presence of God by his throne in heaven. You know, fresh from his presence and glory."

I proceeded to tell Jane that was exactly what I saw in the conference room, that it was not an imaginative vision, that it was real. I told her of the angels smiling at me and writing on the white tablets. After I hung up the phone, I sat in the quiet of the office contemplating what had just happened. It was overwhelming. It was "Mysterium Tremendum," as the theologian Rudolph Otto called God in his splendor. I was totally spent like an old car wash rag. I thought, "Who was I that I might see these powerful, glorious servants of the Living God?"

As I was about to leave the jail, I decided to listen to my phone messages. The first message was from a religious volunteer who lived in Livermore and was a supervisor in a tree trimming and landscaping company. He came to the Santa Rita Jail about once a month. His message on the answering machine was this: "Hi, chaplain. I am just calling to let you know that I prayed for you today that the Heavenly Father would send his angels to you to help you and protect you." I was shocked. This was a second confirmation that these angels were from God, sent to help me.

In the bible, there are several references to these recording "fresh angels" who write in the Book of Remembrances, or Tsdok Zikaron in Hebrew. The angels record our deeds of those who fear God in the Book of Remembrances.[5] In the prophet Ezekiel's vision of the destruction of Israel due to their violence and abominations, God sent six men (angels) with weapons in their hands, and with them "a man clothed in linen, with a writing case at his waist." The man with a "writing case at his waist, brought back word saying, 'I have done as your commanded me.'"[6] The angels I saw had no weapons, but they did write down the proceedings to report back to God on my progress in the face of great opposition by Satan and his followers.

When I returned home that night, I told the full story of my angel encounter and what the two resplendent angels looked like, and the golden aura emitted around their cropped white hair. The best thing about them was their warm and beautiful smiles and penetrating, blazing eyes. My almost three year-old daughter Monika knew about angels from her Children's book of Bible Stories and that Gabriel came to Mary to announce the news that she would be the mother of God. She joined us in the many thank you prayers to the Father God for helping me in this tedious legal matter.

Being a banker and finance person, Jane wondered aloud where we would get the money to pay our legal bills, which were totaling $10,000. I replied confidently, "We can trust God to pay our bills because he sent the angels to be with me, and I am sure he will supply all our needs in his riches in Jesus Christ the Lord." Of course, having made that statement of faith, I had no idea how the Lord would do that, but I did know he was trustworthy. "Faithful is he who had called me, and he will bring it to pass."

I called my mother and Jane's parents to tell them that their prayers had been answered and that the Internal Affairs case was done. My religious volunteers and I celebrated with a potluck dinner

---

[5] Malachi 3:16-17.

[6] Ezekiel 9:2, 11 ESV.

in the conference room next to my office. We even invited some of the Sheriff's deputies. I told them about the angels of God and the great intervention in my life by Jesus the Lord. Sister Overall baked her delicious desserts, and   I brought New Orleans style red beans and rice. We had a feast!

The matter was dropped. It disappeared. Rockne Lucia was elevated in the eyes of his lawyer peers, and Mike Rains let it be known to the Sheriff's Department that he was not to be messed with. Of course, there was still the matter of the large legal bill, but that is another miraculous story. When God says we are his children and the "sheep of his pasture," he means that he will protect us and guide us in this pilgrim way.

Eventually, I did receive a one-sentence email from Sheriff Plummer saying all actions against me are dropped and nothing would be in my file. There was never an apology from him; it was business as usual. The administration treated deputy sheriffs and the chaplain in the same cold-hearted manner. There was never compassion or mercy, just judgment mixed with lies and hypocrisy. It is the way of the world. But the Word of God is my guide. According to James 2:12, "Happy are those who remain faithful under trials, because when they succeed in passing such a test, they will receive as their reward the life which God has promised to those who love him."[7]

---

[7] Two religious volunteers, Randy and Crystal Odom gave me positive affirmations and counsel during the period of time when the Sheriff's department was harassing me with Internal Affairs hearings. They worked with Chinese inmates at North County jail and Crystal was fluent in Mandarin. Randy was a missionary-educator at a university in WuHan China. They pastored a church in Fruitvale area of Oakland, Ca. and now have a ministry at the Church of Three crosses in Castro Valley, Cal.

XVII
Asilomar and Mount Herman

"Even today, the Living God still reigns and speaks to men by direct prophecy when the circumstances demand it and when faith and other conditions are according to his divine will."[1]   H.A. Baker

Ronnie Svenhard is the owner of Svenhard's Swedish Bakery in Oakland. He was the president of the Full Gospel Men's Fellowship and was a great friend of jail and prison ministry. He invited all the chaplains and their wives to a marriage retreat at Asilomar on the Pacific Ocean near Monterey in March of 1997. Jane and I needed a spiritual renewal, so we dropped off our three daughters, Monika and Chloe and Lindsay at the grandparents' house, and we drove down the coast to Pacific Grove. Jane was spiritually exhausted from the constant battles I was having as a chaplain, the financial pressure we were experiencing, along with the spiritual warfare against the "Principalities and Powers of wickedness in high places."

Asilomar was originally a YWCA (Young Women's Christian Association) camp at the end of the 19th century. The camp offered young women retraining in vocations and education providing them career choices other than factory work in large cities. Donated by the Pebble Beach Company, the property faced the ocean on Monterey Peninsula. The first buildings and meeting hall were designed by Julia Morgan, a very famous San Francisco architect. The name, Asilomar, was bestowed by a Stanford University student, Helen Salisbury, in a contest. The name comes from two Spanish words, *asilio* and mar. *Asilio* mean "retreat or refuge," and mar means "sea." The words combined meant "refuge by the sea."[2] The refuge by the sea had a Christian origin and reflects the beauty and creativity of the Creator God. These 30 acres of beach front property were as ideal for retreats and spiritual reflection as they had been for training young women with job skills.

---

[1] H.A. Baker, Visions Beyond the Veil (New Kingston: Whitaker House, c. 1973, 2006) 148.

[2] (<Google.Vistasilomar.com>)

The retreat delivered to us some unexpected and surprising events. On Sunday, the leaders of the retreat asked Jane and me to speak briefly on the struggles we had experienced in prison ministry. Using a baseball analogy, I told the group we were now in the Big Leagues and must be able to hit a 95 mph curve ball. I said, "I believe God is calling us all out of the minor leagues. It is time to grow up, stop complaining or giving in to fear and doubt sown from the devil, and live in the glorious freedom and power of the Lord Jesus Christ." This exhortation surprised me, because I had come to the retreat to receive the Word, not to deliver one.

Jane shared very honestly with the chaplains and their wives saying, "I feel as if I have fallen into a deep hole, and I am trying to bail out as I am sinking in the mire. But I remember God's promises to us through the prophets, Dick and Judy French, that 'God has called us to feed his sheep in the jails and prisons' who are crying out 'We want God! We want God!'" As Jane spoke, I remembered these promises and the vision given to us at Don Wilson's house in Foster City.

The theme of the Asilomar retreat was "Worship and Commitment in Marriage." It was a great blessing to us. Henry and Hazel Slaughter from Nashville, TN, sang and preached under the anointing power of the Holy Spirit. It was a time of spiritual refreshment and revitalization for us as a couple. The Slaughters had great wisdom and humor, and we were blessed. Jane and I took walks along the seashore, watching the sandpipers hunt for insects in the sand with their long, pointed beaks. Seals, Pacific dolphins, and otters swam in the clear, cold waters of Monterey Bay. For Jane, growing up in California, the beach has always been a place of peace and joy, especially Santa Cruz, near Monterey. The conference ended with Holy Communion, and we experienced the "Real Presence of Jesus" in the body and blood of the sacrament. Our retreat at Asilomar was a little taste of heaven.

I was reminded of the missionary to China, H. A. Baker, and his wife, Josephine, who started a home for beggar children in Yunnan Province in a little town called Kotchiu. There, in the late 1920s and early 1930s, they experienced the "latter rains of the Holy Spirit" on the children aged eight to eighteen. The poor, uneducated children saw heaven in visions and were given extraordinary gifts of the Holy Spirit as great as Pentecost in the bible, Acts 2. The young beggar boys and girls met angels and walked around heaven and spoke of this during their prayer times. The missionary couple wrote down the visions and prophecies, many of which concerned the second coming of Jesus Christ. The boys spoke in prophetic authority regarding Jesus. They healed the sick and cast out demons. The author believes that in the last days, the church will have these powers, which have disappeared from the earth. Rev. Baker's description of heaven from the orphans' accounts is as follows:

> "There is a park where birds of all plumage are ever singing; there is a land where every ear will be turned to hear soul-stirring anthems; there is a land where flowers of every hue are forever blooming; there is a land where every eye will be opened to see them in their beauty; there is a land where the fragrances of the Rose of Sharon and the Lily of the Valley mingle with a thousand perfumes that man has never known."[3]

Another spiritual refuge for us was Mount Hermon Conference Center located in the Santa Cruz Mountains at an elevation of 2,000 feet. Mount Hermon was founded in the early 1900s by a group of Presbyterian businessmen as a spiritual retreat. The camp is surrounded by 2,000 year-old Sequoia Redwood trees, remnants of primordial times when dinosaurs roamed the earth. The Pacific Ocean and the City of Santa Cruz are a mere eight miles away.

Since my days as an intern minister at the First Presbyterian Church in San Mateo, I had been coming to Mount Hermon. I loved this special place which angels surrounded and kept watch over. Some of our best memories from my seminary days were from Mount Hermon with Bob Pitman and the saints from the large evangelical church. It was late March of 1997 when Jane and I returned to Mount Hermon. The flowers were blooming, and the ferns were lush and thick under the redwoods, cedars, and pines. Jane and I needed to rest and recover from the latest rounds of spiritual warfare and the usual weariness

[3] Baker, 172.

of raising three daughters. Furthermore, the $10,000 legal bill from Carrol, Burdick, and McDonough law firm pressed heavily on our hearts. Nevertheless, we felt led to go to the retreat, directed by the Holy Spirit.

At the retreat, during dinner, I saw an old chaplain friend, Roland Ruffin. Rev. Ruffin invited us to sit with him for fellowship. Chaplain Ruffin was a veteran of the prison politics and spiritual battles with Satan over the hearts and minds of convicts at Deuel Vocational Institute in Tracy, which coincidentally was where Jane and I currently lived. We began to exchange prison stories of our victories and defeats as chaplains are inclined to do. Jane mentioned how much we were paying in income taxes with no deductions for housing like other ministers had. Alameda County would not separate my wages and housing allotments from my pay. Chaplain Ruffin said, "I work for the State of California, and I write off deductions for housing. I will send you information on my tax specialist, Bob Beeson. He specializes in ministers' taxes, and he will help you." True to his word, he called Jane the next day and gave her the phone number for Beeson's Tax Service. Mr. Beeson met with us and reviewed our taxes for the three previous years, 1994-1996, and filed for back taxes for the housing deduction for ministers and chaplains.

Several weeks later, we received a letter from the Western Regional Offices of the IRS in Ogden, Utah. Inside it was a beautiful green check for $10,600. We praised God. He had not forgotten us. He sent the angels to help us in my legal case, and now he had paid our legal fees in full with enough money left over for a family vacation. That summer we went to Whidbey Island off the coast near Seattle.

To say that "God has your back" does not fully express the love, compassion, and encouragement extended to us, who are grafted into the family of God by the eternal blood covenant of Jesus. I wear a black jacket that a chaplain friend, Robert LittleCloud, ordered for me from the Blackfoot Tribe in Montana. On the back it bears a scripture embroidered in large teal letters: "This is the blood which seals the covenant that the CREATOR has commanded you to obey."[4]

---

[4] Heb. 9:20.

Above the words flies a large bald eagle, a symbol of power to Native Americans.

The prophet Isaiah describes the spirit-filled life in this way:

"He gives power to the faint, and to him who has no might he increases strength. Even youths shall faint and be weary, and young men shall fall exhausted; but they that wait for the Lord shall renew their strength; they shall mount up with wings of eagles; they shall run and not be weary; they shall walk and not faint."[5]

As I walked in the power of the Holy Spirit, I encountered many roadblocks, detours, and dead end paths, but I persevered by the grace of God and the prayers of the saints. My wife, Jane, is a woman of great faith. Though at times she felt I was misguided and stubborn, she believed in the words of prophecy, the visions, and the dreams that the Spirit had spoken to us. She also read through the entire bible and meditated on its truth and wisdom daily. She believed in the Angels' power to care for us and encircle us with protection.

---

[5] Isa. 40:29-31 ESV.

XVIII
A Hedge of Protection

"Have you not put a hedge around him and his house and all that he has, on every side? You have blessed the work of his hands, and his possessions have increased in the land."[1]

After winning my appeal in the Internal Affairs investigation with the help of the "fresh angels," I received a one-sentence note from the Sheriff's Department stating: "All proceedings were dropped, and the letter of the investigation notice would be removed from my file." After a brief celebration party, I wrote this prayer of praise to the Lord God:

"Lord God, how lovely Thou art and your dwelling places, your mansions, and castles! To dwell in Thy presence, to smell the herbs and spices and drink the wine of your Holy Spirit is my delight and joy! To labor in the vineyard of lost souls behind steel bars and to "Lord God, how lovely Thou art and your dwelling places, your mansions, and castles! To dwell in Thy presence, to smell the herbs and spices and drink the wine of your Holy Spirit is my delight and joy! To labor in the vineyard of lost souls behind steel bars and to reap the harvest in the gritty mines below the earth is my task and work for God. How long I toil, who knows? My cup runs over, and the table is set in the presence of my enemies, yet I shall not fear, for you are my Deliverer and Shield, Oh God of Resurrection and life, without end! You have led me by the hand all these years, and I have never gone without food or shelter or clothing. All my needs, Lord Jesus, you have richly bestowed upon my family and me until our cup runs over! And now I pray to the Lord God to lead me into the next millennium with a heart full of praise and a song of victory on my lips. For you, O Lamb of God, have conquered death, and you, Jesus, will return to receive the first fruits of your great sacrifice on the cross for redemption!

---

[1] Job 1:10 ESV.

In my New King James Study Version of *The Open Bible*, the editors list six important, specific duties of Angels' ministries to the Believers:

1. Angels worship God. Matt. 18:10, Rev. 4:8-11 (Living creatures worship at the throne of God, "Holy, Holy, Holy is Lord God Almighty who was and is to come!")
2. Angels protect God's people. Dan. 6:22, Acts 5:19 (Daniel in the lion's den and Peter in prison.)
3. Angels give guidance. Acts 8:26, Acts 27:23 (Guidance given to Philip and Paul.)
4. Angels bring judgment to the wicked. Gen. 19:12-13, Acts 12:23 (Sodom and Gomorrah and Herod the King)
5. Angels ministered to Jesus and helped him. Luke 22:43, Acts 1:11 After temptation by Satan in the wilderness. Mark 1:13
6. Angels accompanied Jesus when he returned to earth. Matt. 24:13; Matt. 13:39, 49, 50; Rev. 21:122[2]

In the summer of 1971, I had a near death experience due to mixing drugs and alcohol. I felt then and believe now that an angel of death had come to take my life as I stood in the farmer's field looking up toward heaven. It was 2:00 a.m. My friends and I were driving in the countryside near Flint. I sensed death all around me and did not want to die in that car. I left the confines of the car and entered the field. My friends thought I was out of my mind, but in that moment of looking up to heaven for help, the death spirit left me, and I suddenly felt well again. Perhaps my mother was praying for my protection, and the angel of the Lord came to me and delivered me from death that night.

Satan used Psalm 91 in an effort to tempt Jesus to leap from the pinnacle of the temple in Jerusalem: "In their hands they shall bear you up, lest you dash your foot against a stone."[3] Of course, the devil omitted verses 15-16: "He shall call upon Me, and I will answer him; I will be with him in trouble; I will deliver him and honor him. With long life I will satisfy him and show him my salvation."

---

[2] *The Open Bible*, NKJ version (Nashville: Thomas Nelson Pub.) 1762.
[3] Ps. 91:12.

Yom Kippur, the Day of Atonement, fell on Monday, September 20, 1999. On this day, the Jews celebrate deliverance from the angel of death and their exodus from the land of Egypt. All leaven is removed from the homes, and a simple dinner of lamb, bitter herbs and spices, unleavened bread, and kosher wine is served. A chair is left vacant for Elijah. The family sings "Next year in Jerusalem." This saying means that the prophet Elijah must return before the Messiah comes. This Passover meal is in remembrance of that time when the angel of death passed over the homes of the Hebrews who had placed lamb's blood on the top and sides of their doorposts. The slaughtered lamb is Jesus whose blood stained the cross, and the prophet of his coming was John the Baptist.

At 4:30 a.m., I awoke fully rested, and I began to read Exodus 23 in the New International Version. I noticed that I had marked several passages with the dates January 2, 1985, and February 4, 1985. The note scribbled next to these verses was "Answer to a morning prayer on God's direction." I remembered my life had been very chaotic at that time. I was about to lose my job at a halfway house counseling convicts and drug addicts. Jane was considering a divorce, which she finally voiced to me on our drive from Los Angeles to Burlingame. She felt that the "marriage wasn't going anywhere," and she was "tired of wandering around. Jane was being honest in her feelings. Satan waged a demonic attack on our weakest point at that time, our marriage. Satan never attacks one's morals first. Rather, he attacks one's joy in Jesus first. John Wesley often talked about the Joy in serving God, but when it departs, Satan tempts us with the sins of the world and the flesh.

When Moses and his people were preparing to fight their enemies on the way to the Promised Land, a verbal promise was made to them: "Behold, I send the Angel before you to keep you in the way and to bring you into the place which I have prepared."[4] I applied this verse to the "giants in the land that I was facing," and I took great comfort from this scriptural promise. During this time, Jane was being attacked even more than me. Eight months after her doubts about our marriage, she

---

[4] Ex. 23:20 NKJ.

was given a vision of the battle raging over us at the time. The record of this event was written in my personal journal in October 1985, shortly before our first daughter was born. I was already asleep, but Jane lay awake. We had just had a "kinship group" meeting with about thirty people from the San Francisco Vineyard Church, which was just forming. Jane recounted to me the 3D color battle scene between the angels and demons that took place above the bed:

> "A horde of evil spirits, demons, were fighting angels above me in the bedroom. The demons were all shapes and sizes with murderous intents to harm us. But the angels were full of light   and the glory of the Lord. They carried the swords of the Spirit.   The demons could not defeat the angel army as they had no heavenly weapons, for they were fallen angels, stripped of the power of heaven and under the curse of God. The battle was not over right away as the two armies fought for an hour!"[5]

As I now reflect on more than forty years of walking in the Spirit and doing spiritual warfare, it is obvious to me that Jesus has put a "hedge of protection" around my family and me. Satan's complaint about the righteous man Job was that the Lord God had put a "hedge around him and his house and all that he has, on every side."[6] Job lived in the land of Uz, which was where the Arameans lived somewhere east of Palestine. He was wealthy with sheep and cattle. The Book of Job, written between 2000-1000 BC, is wisdom literature composed of poetry with parallelism. Much of Job's poetry was apparently passed on in oral form from collected stories. It could very well be the oldest writings in the bible, dating to the time of Abraham and the patriarchs.[7]

The Hebrew word for "hedge" means to "fence up or protect." This same idea is used in Psalms 3:3 and 34:7. In this last Psalm, David writes, "The angel of the Lord encamps around those who fear him, and delivers them." In Psalm 3, David says that God is a "shield around

---

[5] M.S. Lynch, *Journal*, October 1985.

[6] Job 1:10a ESV.

[7] Kenneth Barker and John Kohlenberger III, NIV *Bible Commentary*, vol. 1, Old Testament, 742-743.

me, my glory, the One who lifts my head high." God protects his people from Satan's fiery missiles and the death angel. This does not, however, mean that Christians will not suffer or even die! Paul clearly states, in both 2 Tim. 3:12 and 1 Thess. 3:4 that all who seek to live Godly lives in Christ Jesus will suffer persecution.

In Father Pascal Parente's book, *The Angels*, the priest reminds us that the war in heaven between Michael the Archangel and the fallen angels was not the highest heaven where Jesus dwells with the Father God and Holy Spirit. It was not "the heaven and glory of the Beatific Vision, but the heaven of the spirit world during the period of probation; for no sin is possible in the land of the Blessed nor war in the house of peace."[8] He also states that Satan's chief strategies in destroying human beings are in three areas: seductive temptations of the flesh, diabolical obsessions and possessions, and finally, Black Magic, Spiritism, and the superstitions of idolatry.[9]

About the same time that I was reading and thinking about spiritual warfare and praying for my ministry among the prisoners, a strange thing occurred. I finally had peace from the constant Internal Affairs investigations, and the ministry was flourishing. I began to hear a voice in my head saying, "You are going. You are going." This went on for several weeks, the voice of the Holy Spirit speaking to me. I mentioned it to Randy Levin, one of my faithful jail volunteers at NCJ, and I asked him, "What do you think this means? Does the voice in my head mean I am going to die or that I am leaving the ministry?" Randy said, "I don't know what it means, but you should pay attention!"

---

[8] Pascal Parente, *The Angels in Catholic Teaching and Tradition* (Charlotte: Tan Books, 1994) 61-62.

[9] Ibid., 61.

XIX
Going, Going, Gone!

"Discernment, then, is the process of intentionally becoming aware of how God is present, active, and calling us as individuals   and communities so that we can respond with increasingly greater faithfulness."[1]

Elizabeth Liebert

In 1999, after a year of calm waters, the tempest broke, and the devil attacked me with full force. He used the frail, sinful men at the Sheriff's Department. Sgt. Carmine informed me, "The Sheriff is terminating you on March 6." Dick Delaney, my union representative, was working with SEIU Local 3 attorneys in Oakland. He told me the lawyers from the Weinberg Law Firm were excellent, but the justice system moves slowly, and it would take a year for my case of wrongful termination to be heard. In other words, I had to find another job.

Jane had taken a part-time job in the Tracy Unified School District Gladys Poet Christian School, an elementary school near our house. Two of our daughters were attending the school. I applied for and got a job as a substitute teacher in the district.

On April 24, I attended my daughter Monika's soccer game in Manteca. When I saw Jane, she told me that the Administrative Law Judge, Robert Bryant, had decided in my favor for unemployment compensation. The Alameda County Sheriff's Department had tried to deny me unemployment compensation citing "misconduct." In my journal, I wrote the following regarding the judge's finding:

> "The judge wrote a four-page decision and said that the Alameda County Sheriff's Department should not have denied me my unemployment as the allegations that I had lied were not proven and could not be called misconduct."[2]

---

[1] Elizabeth Liebert, *The Way of Discernment* (Louisville: Westminster John Knox Press, 2008).

[2] M.S. Lynch, *Journal*, April 24, 1999.

The judge went on to quote Maywood Glass Company v. Stewart, a 1959 law case which defined misconduct as "connected with work as a substantial breach by the claimant of an important duty or obligation owed by the employer, willful or wanton in character and tending to injure the employer." The decision concluded that "the claimant was discharged for reasons other than misconduct. Benefits are payable provided the claimant is otherwise entitled to them."

I was elated both by the decision and by the thorough scourging the Sheriff's Department received in the four-page diatribe. The "benefits payable" amounted to a considerable amount of money, which my family desperately needed. I had been to a Christian Missionary and Alliance retreat for pastors in Redding. After the Communion service, there was a time of prayer. I asked for prayer, and three men that I did not know laid hands on me and began to prophecy: "The Lord who took care of the prophet Elijah by the widow of Zarephath with her little oil and flour will do this for you, and the oil and flour will not run out until the rain falls on the earth again."[3] Again, the Lord had met our needs as a family, just as he took care of the widow of the prophet through Elisha by magnifying the olive oil so that she could sell it.

By May of 1999, I had been out of work for 16 months. I worked as a substitute teacher, and Jane worked a 20-hour part-time position at Poet Christian School where Chloe and Lindsay were students. On Sunday, May 9, we were sitting in the Lutheran Church that we had been attending, and Jane began to write feverishly on the youth bulletin. I asked her what she was doing. She said, "God just spoke to me!" "Well, what did he say?" I asked. I read the message she had written down and was flabbergasted.

"Wherever I send you, it must not be with any personal gain in mind, but as a servant with no goals but My goals to reach others. Don't forget the woman who fed the prophet. Wherever you go will be in the spirit of Jim Elliot."[4]

---

[3] 1 Kings 17:8, 16
[4] M.S. Lynch, *Journal*, May 1999

Of course, this message from the Holy Spirit in the middle of church got my attention. I knew that Elisabeth Elliot had written a famous book about Jim Elliot entitled The Savage My Kinsmen. In it, she described his death in 1956 at the hands of Auca Indians. Jim and four other missionary men died with spears in their bodies. Later, Elisabeth went to live with this same tribe, and many of these savage natives became Christians. In June 1999, I wrote the following quote from Elliot's book in my journal:

> "What is a missionary? The word missionary does not appear in the bible. But the word witness does. I found many passages indicating that I was supposed to be a witness. One in particular arrested me. It stated that to be a witness to God is, above all, to know, believe, and understand him.[5] All that He asks us to do is but means to this end! He will go to any lengths to teach us, and His manipulation of the movements of men—Aucas, missionaries, whomever—is never accidental. Those movements may be incidental to the one thing, which He goads us: 'the recognition of Christ.'"[6]

The court orders for my complete reinstatement to the chaplaincy and the payment of all lost wages was handed down by the Administrative Law Judge Robin Matt on May 15, 2000. In his written summation of my case, Judge Matt wrote:

> "In view of my findings that the most serious allegations of willful dishonesty against Appellant and the majority of the other allegations against him are not supported by a preponderance of the evidence on the record, and in consideration of his long service and heretofore satisfactory record of evaluations, I recommend that the appellant's termination be rescinded and that he be reinstated in his position and made whole for any loss of earnings.."

In our Christmas letter dated December 22, 1999, Jane and I wrote the following:

> "The Lord has supplied all our needs in his riches in Christ Jesus! The promise in 1 Kings 17:14-16 of the bread and oil not

---

[5] Isa. 43:10.

[6] Elisabeth Elliot, *The Savage My Kinsman* (New York: Harper Bros., 1961).

diminishing until that famine is over is especially important to us today! Everything is in a constant state of flux, but the Lord does not Change: "He is the same: Yesterday, today and tomorrow." … In a few days, it will be a new millennium. Hopefully it will be a good opportunity to bring some peace, happiness, and joy into an otherwise dark world full of wars and famine. Jesus is the Light of the world, and we pray for his Second Coming in our lifetime! (Shalom, Mike, Jane, Monika, Chloe, and Lindsay)"

The visions and dreams of the great tidal wave of mud and the orange Alameda County dump truck had come to pass, but we were not crushed. Judge Matt ordered that my job as chaplain was to be restored to me and all monies owed to me be "made whole." The Alameda County Sheriff's Department was ordered to pay me nineteen months back pay plus Kaiser medical plus interest. I returned to my position and filled out new paperwork at the personnel office. Then in August of 2000, I decided to accept a teaching position that had been offered to me. This also was fortuitous, because I learned later that the Sheriff and his honchos had been planning to put me on work furlough with nothing to do all day since the prisoners were working in the community. I submitted a one-sentence letter of resignation and never returned to the department.

The other chaplain, Dan, who had done me great harm by telling lies and making innuendoes about me, was charged with 22 counts of child molestation, took a plea bargain, and was sentenced to 16 years in a California state prison. The molestation of three boys occurred between 1983 and 2000.[7] I did not derive any pleasure in this event because he had a wife and small baby at the time. It did, however, bring to mind the prophetic word by Mary's mysterious prophetess in San Carlos just prior to my appointment as a chaplain. She had described a "man with a swollen head like an orange, dripping sweetness, but on the inside, he is vile and not to be trusted." This word of knowledge had been realized in vivid fashion. And my days as a chaplain were over.

---

[7] <(www.oaklandtribune.com/Stories, "Ex-chaplain receives 16 years in molestation." By Jeff Chorney, June 6, 2002.)>

XX
A New Millennium and a New Calling

"When you teach, you change the very order of things from what is to what is possible."   *Leigh Standley, 2012*

On May 6, 2000, I awoke from a very disturbing dream. I arose from my bed and wrote the dream into my journal. The dream was prophetic and terrifying. I believe it is coming to pass even though it has been sixteen years since I experienced this "great dream." This is what I recorded at the time:

"At just before 3:00 a.m., I had a very disturbing dream or vision from God. I was somewhat awake and asleep. In the dream, I remember receiving three pieces of identical mail from Seattle Pacific University in Seattle, Washington. The items were beautiful color brochures, eight by eleven inches, pictures of the student body. Their faces were from all over the world, especially Asia! I was at the school looking at the faces, and my face was there, too!

"Then, in my dream-vision, everything changed and suddenly the Lord God appeared to me and was in my bedroom at my house in Tracy, California. God moved on the winds of the Cherubim, on the wind of the Holy Spirit. He moved by the Spirit in front of me so quickly that He was a blur! The sound of His coming was like that of a roar of a locomotive and an earthquake all at the same time. The message that God proclaimed was truly heartbreaking: 'The sins of your generation and your sins have come before Me, and they are blasphemies and continual rejection of the Lamb of God, Jesus!' In Psalm 18:9-10, He writes: "He rode on a cherub and flew; He came swiftl,y on the wings of the wind." This is how I saw YHWH in my dream.

"These sins were not from evil people in the world, but rather they were from the Church and Believers! My stomach became upset and nausea swept over my whole body. The sins of the people of God were named in a split second, millions of them, and Jesus carried them all on the cross. The Lord God's entrance and exit occurred twice in the dream, and He always moved on the Cherubim from right to left across the bedroom. His sight was too terrible to behold, as God was awesome in power and majesty. Yet, his message was one of repentance, confession of sins, and turning back to Jesus Christ, the Son of God."[1]

In the dream, there was hope for a great world revival coming from young, college age people especially from my alma mater, Seattle Pacific University. The Asian faces in the glossy, colored pictures represented a great move by the Holy Spirit throughout Asia in the last days. The sins of Christians in the West included "unbelief, rebellion, pride, disobedience, mocking, haughty spirit, worship of false prophets, coldness of heart, and quenching of the Holy Spirit in the church." My response to this vision in the night was to pray on my sofa downstairs for several hours in repentance. I asked God for mercy for his people and the church. I meditated on the dream and vision for many weeks and months. I believe we are living in the last days, and "judgment begins in the house of the Lord."

The Eighth Century prophet Amos prophesied to both the Northern and Southern Kingdoms of Israel. It was a time of prosperity for the Israelites, but they also had terrible sins:

"For three transgressions of Israel, and for four, I will not revoke the punishment, because they sell the righteous for silver—those who trample the head of the poor into the dust of the earth and turn aside the way of the afflicted; a man and his father go into the same girl. So that my holy name is profaned; they lay themselves down beside every altar on garments taken in pledge, and in the house of their God, they drink the wine of those who have been fined."[2]

I cannot explain why the Spirit of God gave me this vision. I am not a chaplain not a pastor or even an elder in the church, and yet God

[1] M.S. Lynch, Journal, May 6, 2000

[2] Amos 2:7-8 ESV.

speaks to me as to a prophet and has since I was 20 years old. About prophets, Amos had this to say:

"For the Lord does nothing without revealing his secret to his servants the prophets. The lion has roared; who will not fear? The Lord God has spoken; who can but prophesy?"[3]

In 1922, prior to his conversion to Christianity and the Anglican Church, T.S. Eliot wrote in his famous epic poem "The Wasteland,"

"Who is the third that walks beside you?

When I count, there are only you and I together

But when I look ahead up the white road

There is always another walking beside you

Gliding wrapped in a brown mantle, hooded.

I do not know whether a man or a woman—

But who is that on the other side of you?[4]

Eliot was looking for hope in either Christianity or Hinduism. When he was confirmed in the Anglican Church of England, Christ became his companion on the "white road." He is my favorite poet and was also my mother's poet of choice, along with Helen Steiner Rice.

Since Jane and I were both teachers, we had the summer months off. We planned a family vacation for the months of July and August 2000, to include Michigan, Washington, DC, and New York City. We flew to Detroit and visited my sister Julie, her husband Larry, and their children in Ann Arbor. We rented a Dodge Intrepid and put 3800 miles on it driving in a big loop from Detroit to New York to Washington, DC, and back through Gettysburg to Detroit.

We spent two days in New York City visiting Ellis Island and the Statue of Liberty in the New York harbor. We took some spectacular pictures of the World Trade Center towers above Battery Park. We could not know that in less than two months, both towers would be

---

[3] Amos 3:7-8 ESV.

[4] T.S. Eliot, "The Wasteland," V, lines 360-365.

destroyed by a terrorist group called Al Qaeda. This act of war would plunge us into wars in Afghanistan and Iraq that continue fifteen years later. The attack was planned by Saudi citizens. Iraq had nothing to do with it. I cannot help but think that the 3,000 lives lost in the collapse of the towers was but the beginning of a "time of trouble for America" as prophesied by Nostradamus, the 17th Century seer, who predicted both WWII and a third world war that is yet to happen.

I was at Monte Vista Middle School teaching eighth graders Language Arts and American History when the twin towers were destroyed by two jet liners intentionally crashed into the buildings. The World Trade Center was emblematic of American economic power and prestige, which is why Osama Bin Laden chose it as one focus of his attack on America. His inspiration was not the Quran but rather Satan and the Prince of Persia, a powerful territorial evil spirit.[5]

While I was walking near a lake in Central Park on August 1, 2000, I recorded the following in my journal:

"There is an incredible statue of an angel with wings stretched forth standing over a large fountain near a lake in Central Park. Under the angel's wings are Cherubs by the water where the higher pool spills into a large courtyard pool. The angel is majestic and watches over Central Park in New York City."[6]

The angels watch over all Believers in Christ.

Where were the "eyes of the Lord" that roam about the world seeking those who are upright in heart and love God when 3,000 Americans died on 9/11/2000? God was there, and His cross was over the terrible deaths in Jesus, who died for the sins of the entire world. I am reminded of the "three crosses" revealed to Jane when the Holy Spirit spoke to her. In the center of the cross was God's great love for Jesus and for us, which he demonstrated by dying in our place on the Roman cross in 33 AD. Two days after the bombing of the World

---

5 Daniel 10:10-14. Michael the Archangel defeats the Prince of Persia after a 21-day battle.

6 M.S. Lynch, *Journal*, August 1, 2000.

Trade Center, Jane had a powerful dream about this tragedy, which I recorded in my journal:

"Jane had a dream yesterday that she was in the World Trade Center tower and escaped. She managed to get a cab despite her fear, and in the cab, God spoke to her and said, 'The Church is the only thing that can hold together the threads in this time of world suffering!'"[7]

Matthew records Jesus as saying, "And I tell you, you are Peter, and on this rock, I will build my church…I will give you the keys of the kingdom of heaven, and whatever you loose on earth shall be loosed in heaven."[8] Jesus said that "the gates of hell shall not prevail against it." In theology, this statement by Jesus is called "The ministry of the keys." This ministry is supernatural. It involves prayer, church discipline, pulling down of strongholds, reading the bible, and the means of grace in the Eucharist and Baptism. In 66AD, Paul gave this advice to his protégé Timothy, a young pastor:

"I am reminded of your sincere faith, a faith that dwelt first in your grandmother Lois and in your mother Eunice and now, I am sure, dwells in you as well. For this reason I remind you to fan into flame the gift of God, which is in you through the laying on of hands, for God gave us a spirit not of fear but of power and love and self-control."[9]

This is the ministry of the keys that was given to Peter by Jesus and to all who are overseers in the Church of Christ. The death and destruction in America caused by Islamic Jihadists was prophesied by some American prophets. One of these even had an artist draw on a canvas the vision he had of two towers and a pile of scrap surrounding the devastation. The prophet did not know it was New York City, but he did know it was in America.

In his books, *The Vision and Set the Trumpet to Thy Mouth*, David Wilkerson has long held that America is the "Babylon" of the Book of Revelations in the bible. In 1985, he prophesied:

---

[7] M.S. Lynch, *Journal*, September 13, 2000.

[8] Matt. 16:18-19 ESV.

[9] 2Timothy 1:5-7 ESV

"I believe modern Babylon is present-day America, including its corrupt society and its whorish church system. No other nation on earth fits the description in Revelation 18 but America, the world's biggest fornicator with the merchants of all nations."[10]

Also consider this ancient prophecy made by Nostradamus in the 1600s:

"In the year of the New Century and nine months, from the sky will come a great King of Terror…. The sky will burn at 45 degrees. Fire approaches the great new city…. In the city of York there will be a great collapse, two twin brothers torn apart by chaos while the fortress falls the great leader will succumb. Third big war will begin when the city is burning. The 3rd World War will be greater than the previous two, and 2001 is the first year of the new century and has the ninth month."[11]

In the summer before the events of 9/11, one of my prophetic volunteers, Priscilla Allen, had a powerful dream. She called me in December, and I recorded in my journal what she related to me:

"Priscilla Allen had a prophetic dream last summer before September 11, 2000, attack on America. In the dream, she saw a giant set of plowing discs turn up the soil from the East Coast to the West Coast. The giant plow turned everything upside down, and it came back again from the West Coast to the East Coast. After the soil was tilled, green sprouts shot up higher than a man's head from throughout the country."[12]

Priscilla and Terry, her husband, interpreted the dream to mean that this was the "end time harvest of souls" that results from the catastrophes of the destruction of the cities, i.e., the turning over of the soil. It will begin on the East Coast and spread to the West Coast of the United States.

---

[10] David Wilkerson, *Set the Trumpet to Thy Mouth* (Springdale: Whitaker House, 1985) 3.

[11] <History Channel.com. "Nostradamus parts 1 & 2," November, 2015>

[12] M.S. Lynch, Journal, December 27, 2000.

The prophet David Wilkerson's last great church was on Broadway in New York City. Prior to his death, he wrote:

"I see almighty God even now slowly turning His back on this nation! America is on the verge of committing the unpardonable sin by resisting the Holy Ghost. Soon, there will be repentance only for individuals, but not the nation.... The unthinkable is going to happen to America and parts of Canada, and few will believe it."[13]

---

[13] Wilkerson, 19.

XXI
The School of the Prophets

"We are to stand between the sinning people and their Creator, even as did the prophets of old, and pray for forgiveness."
Agnes Sanford

The San Francisco Theological Seminary is located in San Anselmo, just north of the Golden Gate Bridge and San Francisco in Marin County. The San Anselmo campus is part of the Graduate Theological Union which consisted of ten seminaries. SFTS is the only school having a separate campus. The other nine seminaries are located in the hills above Hearst Avenue and the University of California in Berkeley. According to my philosophy professor, Dr. Walter Johnson, it was the "Acropolis of education." Attending this school had been my goal ever since I changed my major to Biblical Literature and Philosophy at Seattle Pacific University.

In mid August of 1977, Jane and I left a very wet and verdure Washington state for a golden brown state of California in the midst of a severe drought. We moved into a cement bunker-style bungalow of 1950s vintage called Hunter Hall. An entirely cement and rebar construction, including floors and ceiling, it was very quiet. It was heated by electrical coils buried in the cement floor. As we climbed the path up the hill where the seminary chapel and administrative buildings were located, we saw a breathtaking view of Mt. Tamalpais. The seminary had been built on the hill at the turn of the century, and the town of San Anselmo grew around it. Stewart Chapel and the castle-like structure with its round turret next to it reminded me of the Middle Ages. In the library, I was given my own study cariole on the third floor amidst the stacks of books. I put a few personal items on the small desk, and it became my second home for the two subsequent years I spent on campus. I loved reading and meditating on God in that quiet place.

Being a serious student of history, I researched the history of the seminary and its origins. The Presbyterians on the East Coast wanted to have a theological seminary like Princeton Seminary in New Jersey. The first professors to come to California were from Princeton, Harvard, and Yale. They were men of great faith and vision. The buildings on the SFTS campus were named after Drs. Stewart, Montgomery, and Baird. They had long beards and were very serious men who believed in the mission of the church and Jesus' command "to make disciples of all nations baptizing them in the name of the Father, Son, and Holy Spirit, teaching them to observe all that I have commanded you. And behold, I am with you always, to the end of the age."[1] These men of God were trained in Hebrew and Greek and scriptural interpretation as well as missions and evangelism. They would readily ascribe to St. Paul's advice to a young pastor named Timothy:

> "All Scripture is given by inspiration of God, and is profitable for doctrine, for reproof, for correction, for instruction in righteousness, that the man of God may be complete, thoroughly equipped for every good work."[2]

One hundred years later, I entered the "School of the Prophets," as the seminary was called in the book I read. I was initially surprised by this title, but the more I thought about it, the more I appreciated the concept. The original school of the prophets is found in the Elijah-Elisha cycle from 1 Kings 17 through 2 Kings 9. Under my professor Dr. Marvin Chaney, we exegeted portions of the Elijah-Elisha cycle from Hebrew and discussed it. The class was composed of a small group of second year students, which led to interesting discussions. Dr. Chaney was most interested in the sociology of the peasants in Israel and the Northern Kingdom and had written a book about the agrarian society of Israel in the 8th century BC. I and a classmate, Mike Fauser and I were more interested in the "miracle stories."

I was fascinated with the idea that a large group of young men were being trained by the prophets Elijah and Elisha in various cities in

---

[1] Matt. 28:19-20 ESV.

[2] 2 Tim. 3:16-17 ESV.

Israel, including Bethel, Gilgal, and Jericho. The origins of the "School or Company of Prophets" are in 1 Samuel 19:18-24 which recounts how King David fled from Saul and went to see Samuel, the prophet of God, at Ramah. King Saul was trying to kill David, but the Holy Spirit and the prophets were protected by supernatural means:

> "Then Saul sent messengers to take David. And when they saw the group of prophets prophesying, and Samuel standing as leader over them, the Spirit of God came upon the messengers of Saul and they also prophesied."[3]

Saul tried to capture David three times, but the messengers were overcome by the Spirit every time. The prophets were overwhelmed by God's presence and prophesied ecstatically. To use a modern phrase, they were "slain in the Spirit."

The schools of prophets in biblical times offered an alternative avenue of worship to the peasant people and others who had rejected the House of Omri and his evil son, Ahab, who had corrupted the worship of God. Jeroboam had begun the idolatry after God had sent the prophet Ahijah to anoint him king over ten tribes. God had forsaken Solomon and his heirs because they had committed sins and had worshipped Ashtoreh, Chemosh, and Milcom, before whose altars they had sacrificed their children. They had conducted sexual-magical ceremonies in the high places under the trees.

We asked Professor Chaney about the famous story involving a floating axe head. The prophets were conducting a building project along the Jordan River with Elisha as their teacher and prophet. The story tells of an iron axe head that had fallen into the river. The prophet defied the laws of gravity by "cutting off a stick, threw it in there; and he made the iron float."[4] The professor answered by talking about how valuable iron was in a peasant, agrarian society. In other words, the story was folk wisdom, just a myth. I preferred the literal interpretation. I had no problem with God performing miracles in an "open universe" as opposed to a "closed universe."

---

[3] 1 Sam. 19:20 ESV.

[4] 2 Kings 6:5-6 ESV.

During my second year at SFTS, the seminary hired an Evangelical Presbyterian Pastor to be the new Chair of Evangelism, much to my delight. Dr. Don Buteyn came from Hollywood Presbyterian Church and worked with Lloyd Ogilvie, a well-known author and preacher in Los Angeles. He was cut from the same cloth as the professors who called the seminary "the School of the Prophets." I enjoyed the classes on missions and evangelism that I had with Dr. Buteyn. From him, I learned my favorite definition of evangelism: "one beggar telling another beggar where to get the bread." My spiritual classes were from the Jesuits and the Dominicans at the Graduate Theological Union. With Michael Buckley, I studied *Ascent* to Mt. *Carmel* by St. John of the Cross, and Meister Eckhart's *Sermons* with Father Wall.

My brother-in-law's experience in seminary was vastly different from mine. Dale Lusk had attended an evangelical college, Azusa Pacific, a sister school of Seattle Pacific, and then went on to North Park Theological Seminary in Chicago. This was the Evangelical Covenant's denominational school. Jane's parents were Covenant, as was Jane's uncle, the Rev. Vernon Kraft, who officiated at our wedding. Dale had professors who were evangelical in theology and believed that the bible was the written, inspired Word of God for all faith and practice of Christianity. They did not listen for "a Word of God," but rather "the Word of God." Therefore, the context of Dale's theological studies was one of faith in the biblical stories of the prophets, miracles, heaven and hell, angels and devils, and the physical death and resurrection of Jesus Christ as Lord of Lords and King of Kings.

Dale started a missions program in the Covenant Church called Merge Ministries. He began doing this in college at Azusa Pacific. In this missions outreach, Dale trains and sends teams of lay people to Spanish-speaking countries all over the globe. Merge Ministries also has developed an outreach in southern India. The average mission trip is one to three weeks in duration. The individual churches and Christian volunteers pay their own expenses. They do work projects, vacation bible school, and other tasks that the missionaries assign them. On August 2, 2000, Dale visited our home and told us a remarkable story of an encounter he had with an angel on June 21.

Dale was living in McAllen, a border town in southeastern Texas. From McAllen, it is about a three-hour drive to South Padre Island, a resort area on the Gulf of Mexico. Dale took his girlfriend Carmen's fourteen year-old son, James, on a summer outing to the resort to swim and enjoy the white sands of the beach. While James was swimming in the warm waters of the Gulf, he stepped off a ledge. He was not a strong enough swimmer to swim out of the deep water. He began to drown and was yelling for help. James was panicking, struggling in the salt water waves, with no one around to help him. When Dale saw the boy flailing, he swam out to help him. Because James was struggling so violently, Dale was unable to bring him to shore. To avoid drowning himself, he had to abandon the effort and swim back to shore. The young man cried out, "Don't leave me! Don't leave me!" In my journal, I recorded Dale's description of what happened next:

> "All of a sudden, a blonde-haired white man walked past Dale with a surfboard. Dale began to shout out to the young surfer that his friend was drowning. The young man calmly said to Dale, 'Don't worry about him.' Then the young surfer paddled out to James, put him on the surfboard, and swam the drowning boy back to shore towing the surfboard along with him. James was vomiting salt water out of his lungs as he lay upon the beach gasping for air! Dale turned around to thank the blonde-haired surfer, but he had disappeared into thin air."[5]

The hero surfer never spoke to James to inquire whether he was okay, nor did he speak to Dale. He simply vanished. A blonde, Caucasian young man would have been very conspicuous on that beach with mostly brown-skinned Mexicans on vacation. Dale said to me, "The angel of God saved James's life that day on June 21, 2000." I too believe that the man came from heaven on orders from the Lord to save the young boy and then simply vanished.

The angel of the Lord provided a jar of water and prepared two meals of cakes on a coal fire for Elijah the prophet as he was fleeing from the evil Queen Jezebel. The queen put a curse on Elijah's head

---

[5] M.S. Lynch, *Journal*, August 2, 2000.

and sought to kill him for the slaughter of the 450 prophets of Baal. The nation of Israel was on the verge of religious syncretism with idol worship and witchcraft when Elijah ended this false religion on the slopes of Mr. Carmel overlooking the Mediterranean Sea. For this reason, Elijah is considered to be a "second Moses" in Judaism. He saved the nation from destruction by YHWH for idol worship and child sacrifice. But Elijah was flesh and bones and succumbed to a fear that Jezebel would kill him. When he went into hiding, the angels fed him for his "forty days and forty nights journey as far as Horeb, the mountain of God."[6]

Elijah was God's prophet and the head of the school of prophets for 23 years, from 875 BC until his rapture into heaven in 852 BC.[7] Today, if a pilgrim travels to the top of Mt. Carmel, at 10,000 feet there is large statue of Elijah with a flowing beard, sheepskin cloak, and in his right hand the sword with which he slew the prophets of Baal. As great a prophet as he was, Elijah still had fear, doubts, and the wish to die because he tired of carrying the heavy burden of the sinful people of the Northern Kingdom and the ten tribes. In Elijah's last days, knowing that he was about to go to heaven, the college of prophets and Elisha clung to Elijah day and night. Regarding this momentous event, Merrill Unger describes the scene in the hills of Ephraim:

"The faithful prophet's warfare is now accomplished, and God will translate him in a special manner to heaven. Conscious of this, he determines to spend his last moments in imparting divine instruction to, and pronouncing his last benediction on the students in the colleges of Bethel and Jericho. It was at Gilgal— probably not the ancient place of Joshua and Samuel but another of the same name still surviving on the western edge of the hills of Ephraim—that the prophet received the divine intimation that his departure was at hand."[8]

---

[6] 1 Kings 19:8 NKJ.

[7] Carl Unger, *Unger's* Bible Dictionary (Chicago: Moody Press, 1970) 303-305.

[8] *Ibid.*, 305.

On the front door post of my house hangs a wooden sign with an angel carved on it. It says, "Do not fear—the angels are near." For Jane and me, it is not a mere decoration but a reality in our marriage of more than 40 years. Even before our marriage, the angels seemed to have watched over Jane's family and my own. In his theology of the Reformation in 1532, John Calvin wrote:

> "…The angels are dispensers and administrators of God's beneficence toward us. For this reason, Scripture reveals that they keep vigil for our safety, take upon themselves our defense, direct our ways, and take care that some harm may not befall us…."[9]

Calvin believed that we have many angels that assist us as Christians and not just one guardian angel. He also said that God "not only promises to take care of us but tells us he has innumerable guardians whom he has bidden to look after our safety; so that as long as we are hedged about by their defense and keeping, whatever perils may threaten, we have been placed beyond all chance of evil."[10]

As a very young child, I witnessed the truth of being "hedged about" by angels. It was the summer of 1953. My family had just moved to a new home in a housing tract built by my school friend's father, Mr. Schlosser. All the homes were single story, three bedrooms, one bath, wood frame with wood shingles. We lived at 1321 Transue Street between Flint and Davison in Flint. I was a toddler of two and a half years, but I was fully capable of running around in the fields catching butterflies. I had been cooped up in an apartment on a busy street in the city, but at last I was free to roam in the fields and woods behind our house.

On June 8, 1953, the sky turned inky green-black, and the rain was falling in sheets. It was very humid and still. We had just finished dinner, and we knew a big storm was coming. Lapeer Road began to fill up with cars, which we thought was strange for a Saturday. There were

---

[9] John Calvin, *The Institutes of the Christian Religion,* book 1, xiv, 6, ed. by John T. McNeill, trans. by Ford Lewis Battles (Philadelphia: Westminster Press, 1960) 166.
[10] *Ibid.,* 171.

no sirens, no warnings on the radio or television. As we looked out the large picture window in our front room, we saw, much to our horror, a massive tornado bearing down upon us. It was a half mile away, but it seemed to fill the entire horizon. My father told us to get down on our knees and pray because it was too late to try to escape and there were no basements in our area.

I will never forget my father reciting the 23rd Psalm of David: "Yea, though I walk through the valley of the shadow of death, I will fear no evil; for you are with me; your rod and staff, they comfort me." Suddenly, this half mile wide F-5 tornado bypassed our house by lifting over our neighborhood and setting down just east of us, destroying all the houses and businesses along Coldwater Road to the north and east of us. At the time, it was the only F-5 tornado to ever hit Michigan and the ninth largest to ever occur in the United States. The tornado killed 109 people and injured 650 others. Warning sirens were not installed in Flint until after this event. The Flint Journal Newspaper called it "The Finger of God." This monster tore up property and homes for 28 miles through Genesee County.[11]

As a very young child, I witnessed the hand of God in our deliverance from the killer tornado. It made a deep impression. I watched as the funnel cloud lifted back up in the air over our house as my father and mother prayed Psalm 23. I believe the angels of God put a "hedge of protection about us" because we were in the providence and election of God Almighty.

I began this memoir with my mother's dramatic rescue by the Spirit of God at the Denver amusement park in 1942. This was not luck or a fluke event. The Psalmist states this about God's protection of the Saints:

"Behold, the eye of the Lord is on those who fear him. On those who hope in His mercy. To deliver their soul from death, and to keep them alive in famine. Our soul waits for the Lord; He is our help and our shield. For our heart shall rejoice in Him. Because we

[11] <Flint History, 1953, "The Killing Wind".com>

have trusted in his holy name. Let your mercy O Lord, be upon us, just as we hope in You."[12]

These ancient promises from 3,000 years ago are not relics of the past. They are alive and active, "sharper than a two-edged sword." The Holy Spirit points us to Jesus, the mediator of the new covenant in his blood. The text of the bible is illuminated to our hearts by the Spirit of God. "Faith comes by hearing and hearing by the Word of God."[13]

The miracles, signs and wonders, and angels are all edifying to one's spirit and soul, but they do not bring a person into union with God. They are like signposts along the narrow road that points to Jesus as "the way, the truth, and the life." My intent in writing this non-fiction book was to glorify Jesus that "he might increase and I might decrease." The way of the prophet is a lonely path full of obstacles, spiritual warfare, and rejection. "Behind all of the prophet's training runs one basic theme—death of self in order that unity may blossom and the prophet may enable others to shine."[14]

To follow Jesus is to pick up the cross daily. Our death in Christ to our flesh and ego is but the beginning of the path into the Kingdom of God. The deeper things of God belong to those who are persistent and are called to follow Jesus without reservation. By this, I do not mean making an intellectual assent to Jesus' birth, death on the cross, and resurrection from the dead. This is called "conversion or being born from above." Concerning the deeper life in the Holy Spirit, I mean "Union with God." Our personality is not dissolved into the Godhead. It remains with us, but our spiritual eyes are opened to the light of God all around us. Agnes Sanford called this the "healing light." The unknown author of the Middle Ages classic, *The Cloud of Unknowing*, wrote of contemplation in this way:

"Contemplative prayer is God's gift, wholly gratuitous. No one can earn it. It is in the nature of this gift that one who receives it, receives

---

[12] Ps. 33:18-22 NKJ.

[13] Rom. 10:17 NKJ.

[14] John and Paula Sandford. *The Elijah Task* (Plainfield: Logos International, 1977) 63.

also the aptitude for it.... He who experiences God working in the depths of his spirit has the aptitude for contemplation and no one else. For without God's grace, a person would be so completely insensitive to the reality of contemplative prayer that he would be unable to desire or long for it, no more and no less. But you will never desire to possess it until that which is ineffable, and unknowable moves you to desire the ineffable and unknowable."[15]

Dag Hammarskjold, the Secretary General of the United Nations during the mid 1950s and early 1960s, wrote in his diary, "The lovers of God have no religion but God alone." He wrote this diary in 1955, and six years later, on September 18, 1961, he died in a plane crash near Ndola, Northern Rhodesia. He was a Christian and a mystic who gave his life to his fellow man. His book, *Markings*, records his spiritual journey into the "Ineffable and Unknowable."

I read this book at the beginning of my seminary journey so many years ago, but it still speaks to me today. Hammarskold's diary reminds me of my diaries and markings. He said this regarding our spiritual pursuit of God: "So long as you abide in the Unheard of, you are beyond and above—to hold fast to this must be the first commandment in your spiritual discipline."[16] This is very similar to C.S. Lewis's concept of the deeper life in God as "higher up and farther in."

Jane had a remarkable vision in the summer of 1999. It describes the Prophet Elijah and the two altars, one to the pagan god Baal and the other to YHWH, or I Am that I Am. I recorded it in my journal a year later when she reminded me of it:

"Jane reminded me of a vision she had of two altars: one to Baal and the other to YHWH. The altar to the Lord was overflowing with water—three fold—but the altar to Baal had nothing going on despite 450 priests cutting themselves and shedding their own blood! Jane believes that, just as in the days of Elijah and his contest with the false prophets and pagans, so too we must choose which

---

[15] William Johnston. *The Cloud of Knowing* (New York: Doubleday, 1973) 91.

[16] Dag Hammarskjold, *Markings*, trans. by Leif Sjoberg and W.H. Auden (New York: Alfred A. Knopf, 1977) 101.

God to serve. Jesus, the high priest and Lord of heaven, has an altar made from his own blood and flesh sacrifice, which is the acceptable altar that is consumed by the fire from heaven. This fire is God's Holy Spirit consuming the wood, water, and the stone! The other altar to the false god is dead with no sacrifice and no power!"[17]

The markings in this book are from my journal and diary entries that reflect my experience with God: Father, Son, and Holy Spirit. I am not proclaiming this way to be what every Christian should aspire to. The Holy Spirit gives gifts according to his will. My gifting is from the Spirit of God in the areas of dreams, visions, prophecies, etc. I am not a healer like Agnes Sanford nor an evangelist like Billy Graham. I was a chaplain to the incarcerated and a teacher of English and History to middle school students, but I strove to let "God's light so shine in the world that they would see my good works and glorify my Father in heaven." I also spoke the truth in love about Jesus healing us from our sins and coming back again to receive us into his Kingdom.[18] I would hope that people would say of me C'est un homme tres recueilli, "He is a very contemplative man," a man given to prayer and action in Christ. Jeremiah, the weeping prophet, is the model of recueillement and action. His counsel to Israel is good advice to Christians today: "Stand in the ancient ways and see, and ask for the old paths, where the good way is, and walk in it; then you will find rest for your souls...."[19]

My good friends, the prophets Terry and Priscilla Allen, once gave me a plaque from the Morris Cerrullo World Evangelism that I kept hanging in my office at North County Jail. It helped me greatly when I felt defeated by the enemy. The plaque proclaims in raised gold letters:

---

[17] M.S. Lynch, *Journal*, July 12, 2000.

[18] John 14:6.

[19] Jer. 6:16-17 NKJ.

GOD SAID

Don't look to the bigness of your need
Look to the bigness of your God!
Your circumstances are Hindrances to seeing:
MY ABILITIES…

IF YOU KEEP YOUR EYES ON YOUR CIRCUMSTANCES,
THE DEVIL WILL USE YOUR CIRCUMSTANCES TO DEFEAT
YOU AND ACCUSE THE WORD OF GOD…THE WRITTEN
AND THE LIVING WORD.

YOUR VICTORY
Is in keeping your eyes on the bigness of your God and his ability!

HE HAS PROMISED
To take you STEP by STEP…
Not all at once…
But STEP…
By STEP and…

EACH STEP WILL BE A MIRACLE!

Morris Cerullo World Evangelism

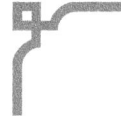

BIBLIOGRAPHY

Adler, Mortimer J. *The Angels and Us*. New York: McMillan Publishing Co., 1982.

Baker, H.A. *Visions Beyond the Veil*. New Kensington: Whitaker House, 1973, 2006.

Barker, Kenneth, and John Kohlenberger, III. NIV *Bible Commentary, Vol. 1*, Old Testament.

Bauer, Walter, trans. William F. Arndt and Wilbur Gingrich, eds. *A Greek-English Lexicon of the New Testament and other Early Christian Literature*. Chicago: University Press and Zondervan Press, 1957.

Brown, Peter. *Augustine of Hippo*. Berkeley: University of California Press, 1967, 1975.

Bullinger, Heinrich. "Second Helvetic Confession," *UPC USA The Book of Confessions*. New York: General Assembly Interchurch Center, 1970.

Calvin, John. *The Institutes of the Christian Religion, Vol. 2*. Edward R. Robinson, ed. Ford Lewis Battles, trans. Philadelphia: The Westminster Press, 1960.

Cerullo, Morris. *The Prophet's Mantle*. San Diego: Morris Cerullo World Evangelis, 2000.

Eckhart, Meister. Raymond B. Blakney, trans. *Meister Eckhart*. New York: Harper and Row, 1941.

Eliot, T.S. *The Waste Land, New York*: Horace Liveright, 1922.

Elliot, Elisabeth. *The Savage My Kinsman*. New York: Harper Bros., 1961.

Frost, Robert. Edward Cunnery Lathem, ed. *The Poetry of Robert Frost*. New York: Rinehart and Winston, 1967.

Godwin, Malcolm. *Angels: An Endangered Species*. New York: Simon and Schuster, 1990.

Graham, Billy. Angels: *God's Secret Agents*. Garden City: Doubleday and Company, 1975.

Hammarskjold, Dag. Leif Sjoberg and W.H. Auden, eds. *Markings*. New York: Alfred A. Knopf, 1977.

John of the Cross. E. Allison Peers, ed. *Ascent of Mr. Carmel*. New York: Image Books—Doubleday and Company, 1958.

Johnston, William, ed., *The Cloud of Unknowing*. (New York: Doubleday, 1973.

Krailsheimer, A.J., trans., *Pascal Pensees*. Baltimore: Penguin Books, 1966.

Liebert, Elizabeth . The *Way of Discernment*. Louisville: Westminster John Knox Press, 2008

Moe, Olaf. The Apostle Paul. Trans by L.A. Vigness, Minneapolis: Augsburh zpub.,House, 1954

Nouwen , Henry J. M. A Cry for Mercy. Syracuse: Image, 2002.

Parente, Pascal. *The Angels in Catholic Teaching and Tradition*. Charlotte: Tan Books, 1994.

Pascal, Blaise. Honor Levi, trans. *Pensees and Other Writings: The Memorial Fragment*. Oxford: Oxford Press, 1995.

Pope, Hugh. "Guardian Angel," The Catholic Encyclopedia, Vol. 7.

Rienecker, Fritz, and Cleon L. Rogers, *Linguistic Key to the Greek New Testament*. Grand Rapids: Zondervan, 1982.

Robinson, Edward R., trans. Francis S. Brown, S.R. Driver, and Charles A. Briggs, eds. *Hebrew and English Lexicon of the Old Testament*. Oxford: Clarendon Press, 1977.

Rohr, Richard. *Falling Upward*. Hoboken: Jossey-Bass, 2011.

Sanford, Agnes. *The Healing Gifts of the Spirit*. New York: Harper Collins, 1984.

Sandford, John and Paula. *The Elijah Task*. Plainfield: Logos International, 1977.

Sandford, John and Paula. *The Transformation of the Inner Man*. Plainfield: Bridge Publishing, 1982.

Spurgeon, Charles. *The Treasury of David, Vol. 1*. Peabody, Hendrickson, 1988.

Stoesz, Samuel J. *Sanctification, An Alliance Distinctive*. Camp Hill:Camp Hill: Camp Hill Christian Publishing, 1992.

Teresa of Avilla. Kieran Kavanaugh and Otilio Rodriguez, trans. *Interior Castle*. New York: Paulist Press, 1979.

Torrey, R. A. *The Person and Work of the Holy Spirit*. Grand Rapids: Zondervan Pub., 1974.

Tozer , A.W. *Keys to the Deeper Life*. Grand Rapids: Zondervan Pub., 1959.

Tozer, A.W. Gerald B. Smith, ed. *The Tozer Pulpit, Vol. 2*. Camp Hill: Christian Publications, 1994.

Wagner, Peter, and Douglas Pennoyer, eds. *Dark Angels*. Ventura: Regal Books, Gospel Light, 1990.

West, Jessamy, ed. *The Quaker Reader*. Wallingford: Pendle Hill Publishing, 1992.

Wilkerson, David. *Set the Trumpet to Thy Mouth*. Springdale: Whitaker House,1985.

Williams, J. Rodman. *The Gift of the Holy Spirit Today*. Plainfield: Logos International, 1980.

BIBLES AND SPIRITUAL PUBLICAITONS

Aland, Kurt, Matthew Black, Carlo Martini, Bruce Metzger, and Allan Wikgren, eds. *The Greek New Testament*, 3rd ed. New York: American Bible Society, 1966.

Book of Common Prayer. New York: The Church Pension Fund, 1945.

Hymnal of Worship and Celebration, #258. Waco: Word Music, 1986.

The Holy Bible, English Standard Version. Wheaton: Crossway Bibles, 2007.

The Open Bible, New King James Version. Nashville: Thomas Nelson Publishing, 1997.

Unger, Carl. *Unger's Bible Dictionary*. Chicago: Moody Press, 1970.

OTHER

<[*lostamusementparks.org/articles/elitchgardens.html*]>

<Flint History, 1953, "The Killing Wind".com>

<Thomas Merton, Thoughts in Solitude, yahoo.comImageResults>

<Google.Vistasilomar.com>

<www.oaklandtribune.com/Stories, "Ex-chaplain receives 16 years in molestation." By Jeff Chorney, June 6, 2002.>

<History Channel.com. "Nostradamus parts 1 & 2," November, 2015>

POSTSCRIPT

Five years have passed since I wrote this book and it was published in 2017 and now it has been refurbished with a section of pictures of my family and friends to complement the story. This book was intended to be be nonpolitical as my mentor Dr. Robert A. Pitman always maintained that "the pulpit should not be used for political purposes." Sadly, in the Evangelical churches this mandate has not always been followed! I believe the great twentieth century theologian, Karl Barth, had it right when he said "the Bible should be read on one hand and the newspaper on the other hand."

I would like to dedicate this book to the memory of a dear Christian brother, Dave Feaver, who died in a tragic automobile accident in October, 2022. I will miss him as we did some woodworking projects for his sailboat and park bench for his wife Irene. God gave me this reading from Psalm 90:12 after his death. "Teach us to number our days aright, that we may gain a heart of wisdom." I am glad to have kept a journal for forty five years and hopefully I have attained a little wisdom from from the inspired Word of God and His Presence in my life and my family and brothers and sisters in the KOINONIA FELLOWSHIP.

Author: M. S. Lynch
Email: lopearjack@gmail.com

M.S. Lynch became a Christian at age twenty while attending Western Michigan University. Following his radical conversion, Mike transferred to Seattle Pacific University where he majored in Biblical literature and philosophy. It was at Seattle Pacific that the author was introduced to the Christian Mystical tradition. This tradition corresponded to his earlier experiences with the Holy Spirit as a young believer and gave validity to his spirituality. Mike worked in several Presbyterian churches in Seattle and in San Mateo, Ca. His Master of Divinity degree was from San Francisco Theological seminary where he studied with Jesuit and Dominican teachers on St. John of the cross and Meister Eckhart. Michael worked as a chaplain with the Alameda Co. Sheriff's department at North Co. jail and Santa Rita jail from 1988-2000. He also was a teacher of language arts and American history in a large middle school in Tracy, Ca. for fifteen years. He is married to Jane Lynch who was greatly instrumental in the writing of the book. Michael has three grown daughters and four grandchildren. He is an active member of the Modesto Covenant Church where he resides in Modesto, Ca.

www.ingramcontent.com/pod-product-compliance
Lightning Source LLC
Chambersburg PA
CBHW051314120626
46547CB00015B/2225